EXTENDING THE CALL

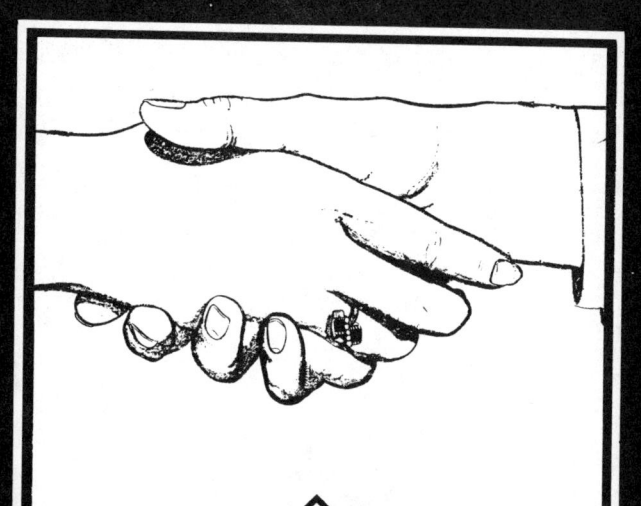

EXTENDING THE CALL

Testimonies of Ordained Women

**EDITED BY
CAROL ANDERSON ANWAY**

Herald Publishing House
Independence, Missouri

Copyright © 1989
Herald Publishing House
Independence, Missouri
Printed in the United States of America

94 93 92 91 90 89   1 2 3 4 5 6

Table of Contents

Introduction 9
Diane Akers 13
Wanda Andersen 15
Sheri Ashley 19
Margaret Athey 23
Anita Ruth Bates 26
Floy L. Bennett 28
Jean (Hawkins) Broadaway 32
Denise Marie (Campbell) Buscavage 36
Vivian Collins Campbell 40
Ethel (Boswell) Carlile 44
Mary Jane Carter 48
Elizabeth (Bettye) Day Cervola 52
Jeanne M. (Benson) Chase 55
Carley J. (Knisley) Cole 59
Lori Combs 63
Linda L. (Troyer) Comstock 67
Joann Condit 71
Elaine Constance 75
Lois Marie Davis 79
Edith Joy (Parker) Dawson 82
Melba Jean Dixon 86
Florence (Toovey) Dreher 89
Emily Dunsdon 92
Carol L. Ergo 96
Genevieve (Hougas) Francis 101
Ruth Midgorden Goodwin 105
Charlotte D. Gould 109
Katherine (Snively) Gregory 115
Janice (Dandurant) Hawman 119

Barbara McFarlane Higdon 123
Sue (Kolquist) Jannetta 129
Lois (Richards) Kazyaka 133
Ardith Lancaster 136
Evelyn Maples 139
Sue (Clements) Massa 143
Brenda M. Mitchell 146
Elaine (Carson) Olson 149
Florence Sanford Ourth 154
Leslie Palmer 157
Amy Evelyn Robbins Parks 161
Jean Porter 163
Jean S. Reiff 166
Geneva Hunker Richards 169
Mary Kathryn (Becker) Richardson 172
Linda Hansen Rounds 176
Virginia (Bean) Schrunk 179
Gael Lynn Self 182
Karen A. Smith 186
Rosaleene (Coumerilh) Smith 190
Marilyn Suddaby 192
Janice M. Townsend 197
Ruby L. Ward 202
Maralin (Miller) Weide 207
Dorothy M. Wolf 209
Peggy (Nikel) Young 212
Frances Zender 218

"It is my will that my priesthood be made up of those who have an abiding faith and desire to serve me with all their hearts, in humility and with great devotion...

"I have heard the prayers of many, including my servant the prophet, as they have sought to know my will in regard to the question of who shall be called to share the burdens and responsibilities of priesthood in my church.

"I say to you now, as I have said in the past, that all are called according to the gifts which have been given them. This applies to priesthood as well as to any other aspects of the work.

"Therefore, do not wonder that some women of the church are being called to priesthood responsibilities. This is in harmony with my will....

"Remember, in many places there is still much uncertainty and misunderstanding regarding the principles of calling and giftedness. There are persons whose burden in this regard will require that considerable labor and ministerial support be provided. This should be extended with prayer and tenderness of feeling, that all may be blessed with the full power of my reconciling Spirit."

Doctrine and Covenants 156:8-10

Introduction

November 15, 1985, was a long-awaited day for many members of the Reorganized Church of Jesus Christ of Latter Day Saints. This was the Sunday when the first women called to the priesthood were ordained. What a celebration it was for those of us who were the friends, relatives, and supporters of those women. Not only members of the church shared in the celebrations, but friends of the church also felt joy with us. And in the days and months that followed, many more women received their calls and their services of ordination were celebrated.

Now, five years after President Wallace B. Smith opened the way for women to be ordained through his inspired document to the 1984 World Conference which became Doctrine and Covenants 156, more than 2,000 women have been called and ordained.

The joy many have felt has not been without anguish, for to some it marked a time of separation from the church. Yet story after story is told of those who, as they struggled with the issue, came to a realization of God's movement in this act. They now share in accepting their sisters' callings.

Women have been ordained in some denominations for a long time; others have begun only recently; it's a "hot" topic in the rest. *Newsweek* magazine recently reported that about 21,000 women have been ordained in approximately eighty denominations in North America. Our experience in the RLDS Church places us in the "first generation" of understanding and acceptance. Perhaps because we view ordination as the public beginning of servant ministry, our congregations (sometimes referred to as branches) have the potential to become a unique expression of the body of Christ.

Most ordained ministers in the church serve as volunteers while maintaining full- or part-time jobs elsewhere. Almost all of the paid ministers are World Church "appointees" or executives.

Although a call may be felt strongly by an individual, it is not something he or she can request but is initiated by a pastor (or presiding elder) in response to the movement of the Holy Spirit. Approval is sought first through administrative channels and then from the individual before being presented for a congregational vote. Ordination is arranged once the individual completes several study courses through Temple School, the church's adult education arm.

These stories have many similar threads—particularly the experience of growth, response, and anticipation. But there are so many variations. Some women received an indication of their call many years before it was received through official channels and who, in wonderment, quietly anticipated the time. Others thought the whole idea silly—wanting nothing to do with it—yet experienced within themselves a change of heart as they felt God's call extended to them. There were those who had sensed no inkling that they would be called. They were preoccupied by their dedicated service to God and happy that others would be called—surely not themselves.

Some women received complete support in their families and congregations. Others had little support from families, and some saw members of their congregations walk out and disassociate themselves.

These testimonies have come from among the first 750 women called, primarily in the United States and

Canada. They have been joined by sisters throughout the world. Letters were sent by the Women's Ministries Commission in cooperation with the History Commission to collect stories to be included in church archives for future research. More than 200 women responded with written testimonies ranging from one to fifteen pages. Editors at Herald House agreed they were too powerful to keep hidden away in the archives. They need to be read and savored by us, to inspire and help us appreciate the quality of dedication among the Saints.

The women also express their history, conversion experiences, points of growth, and frustrations. They remind us of our own life experiences. They bring fresh insights into what ministry is all about. And they renew the importance of our basic call as members of the body of Christ—that each of us is empowered by God as ministers to share our gifts for the purpose of nurturing those around us as we travel together on our spiritual journey.

These are the first testimonies. As the call to serve is extended, let us celebrate them and those which inevitably will follow.

Carol Anderson Anway

Diane Akers
Seattle, Washington

Especially since my ordination as a teacher, I've been awed by the way God's love opens people to share their hurts and needs. At the same time, it has been one of the hardest times for me personally. My husband divorced me, at least in part because of his opposition to women in the priesthood. Yet I have been sustained with the assurance of divine grace.

During the 1984 World Conference my daughter-in-law called to inform me of the revelation. I will never forget the two distinctive feelings I felt as she told me: elation and humility. I remember laying my head on my kitchen cupboard and crying with joy! Without a doubt I knew it to be of God.

Later that following summer, as I was reading the scriptures, the Holy Spirit came in such power that I stood up. The words came to me, "Diane, you are called to my work. You are part of my body; you are my hands and feet." I felt the Spirit pour through me—it was wonderful. I shared this experience with my daughter because I wanted someone else to know about it. She agreed not to tell anyone; I wanted to let the Spirit work through the proper channels to bring it about.

Even though my pastor said he would not call any women, I continued to do the things I felt the Lord was calling me to do. In the spring of 1986, however, a new pastor informed me of my priesthood call. My husband, who was neither in the priesthood nor believed the revelation was divine, asked me to delay my answer for two months. During this time he tried to discourage me, but I had no answer but yes.

The Lord Jesus has always been very real in my life even though I wandered from the Lord's way for several years in my late teens. I'm particularly thankful for parents, grandparents, teachers, and priesthood members who have been instrumental in sharing Christ with me. Through times when I felt completely destroyed by hurt and tragedy, I have come to rely on my Lord. And now, since my ordination, I have found a strength and love for God more profound than I knew before.

Jesus Christ is my closest friend. Many times when I have cried out in despair, his comforting Spirit has been there. Many times when my heart has overflowed with joy, that same Spirit was there as well. That Christ is *always* with me is a promise I can believe in. It's been proven in my life.

I've been involved in many areas of church work: Sunday school teacher, women's leader, treasurer, secretary, women's commissioner, youth exchange director, and camp cook. I have cooked for many camps and reunions over the past fifteen years, and it keeps getting better. I thoroughly enjoy it—never once have I considered it work.

Since my ordination, I have come to believe that ordained teachers carry a unique responsibility: to bring the lost, lonely, and hurt back into the fold. A ministry of healing without administration can come through listening, touching, and caring. We can assist the elders in being healing agents in the world. Together we can be like a desert oasis—a watering place for thirsty souls.

Wanda Andersen
Pittsburgh, Pennsylvania

It was difficult for me to accept the idea of women being called to the priesthood long before it became a reality. I, too, expressed the feeling, "Women have ministered for years without priesthood. Why do they need it now?" Like many other women, I have contributed to the work of the church; my ministry has been well accepted by those with whom I have worked.

I had struggled with this for some time and listened to the pros and cons but was quite disturbed and even cried when it came before the Conference as a revelation.

During the year following approval of Section 156, I listened to testimonies of others who had been having the same struggles I was having but who had received convincing experiences. I also asked friends who had been called to share their testimonies with me. Because of the power of the Holy Spirit that seemed to accompany their experiences, I began to feel that the revelation must be from God. And so I felt I could support the women who had been called in their ministry. But I was perfectly content to minister in the "office of member."

I attended as many Temple School classes as possible in my area, eager to learn and become better equipped to witness. All the time I was hoping my pastor would not feel I was anticipating a priesthood call. I assured those who were discussing women in the priesthood in my presence that I was happy serving as I was and had no interest in being in the priesthood.

The first Sunday in August 1986, my pastor took me aside and told me about my call to the office of teacher. I expressed some of my feelings with him and told him I would have to have a testimony of my own before I could accept the call. He asked me to take some time to think and pray about it and let him know my decision before the business meeting in two weeks. I appreciated his supportive attitude.

A couple of days later he stopped by the house to share more of the details of my call and see how I was feeling. I had written down a long list of reasons why I didn't feel I needed to be in the priesthood. He encouraged me to think more positively and try to see what opportunities priesthood service might bring. I later tried to write some positive reasons for accepting the call but had trouble thinking of any.

I certainly wanted to do whatever God wanted. There was no question I would accept the call if I could get rid of my negative feelings. My pastor's experience helped, but I still felt the need for my own testimony. I reminded myself that lots of calls were accepted on faith, but my faith seemed to be so weak.

I dug out all the books on prayer I could find and at the same time searched for scriptural promises. I thought that if God could let my pastor know about the call (as well as another person who had received confirmation), I just had to *expect* to hear, too.

I began to study, pray, and fast in different ways. I didn't know exactly how to pray to get the answer or how long it would take. I was prepared to pray for a long time, if necessary. First, I prayed rather generally that God would show me in some way that this was his will. Then, when that didn't seem to work (I was getting impatient), I thought I'd try another suggested approach and prayed specifically for confirmation through another person who I knew was having a difficult time with the concept of women in the priesthood. That way we would both have a testimony. Finally, I decided it probably was best to leave it up to God to decide how and when.

I understood that I had up to a year before I gave my pastor an answer. But, because Dick and I are always subject to move at any time as a World Church appointee couple, God must need someone now to work in the office of teacher in our present congregation. So why was it taking so long to get an answer? During all my soul-searching, I finally concluded that God just might be having trouble getting through to me because I was not only struggling with my call but also with the whole issue of women in the priesthood. I had accepted it with my head, but I hadn't really accepted it with my heart.

As I was working at the kitchen sink about three months later, my thoughts were on the new visiting program I hoped to organize as congregational pastoral care commissioner. I had just finished saying to myself, "I don't need to be in the priesthood to do this," when suddenly my thoughts were interrupted. It was as if someone were telling me, "You need to accept the call." At the same time, I received a strong feeling of joy—like I'd never felt before and really can't describe. All my negative feelings began to leave. The awareness of extreme joy and the knowledge that the negative feelings were gone alternated several times during this experience. My eagerness to accept the call was so opposite from my previous feelings that I knew the Holy Spirit was working within me as an answer to my prayers and fasting.

In spite of this positive experience, I decided I wouldn't tell my husband or the pastor yet. I would wait a week and see if the negative feelings returned. If they did not, I would know for sure it was from God.

The next day I realized I had been rebelling. The confirmation I had been seeking had come in a way I never could have imagined and with a power I never before had experienced. I determined then that I would accept the call and tell my pastor on Sunday. There was no longer any doubt in my mind that God wanted women in the priesthood or that my call was from God.

I've been reminded of several things through this whole struggle: (1) God will answer even though we "only desire to believe" and may not feel our faith is strong enough; (2) patience is sometimes needed; (3) God can use us even when we are rebellious (perhaps without realizing it); and (4) God can bend our will if we are willing to let it happen.

Sheri Ashley
Troy, Michigan

When I first read Section 156 a spirit of peace bore assurance to me that it was of God. The portions on the Temple were especially powerful. But my reaction to the part about ordination for women was a deep sadness. I remember thinking, "God, I wish you hadn't done this. I was hoping you never would."

For years I had struggled with the concept of women's ordination. I didn't know if it was God's will nor had I done any serious study of the matter. At one point I reconciled myself to the idea that God did not choose to ordain women, and I was content to minister as I had always done. I had many meaningful outlets for my services and functioned according to my gifts in most other ways.

The potential burden of a priesthood call weighed so heavily on me after April 1984 that for many months afterward I struggled with the divinity of the revelation. My initial experience of divine confirmation was set aside as I agonized over whether or not this could possibly be God's will for the church. I lived with confusion and "stupor of thought" (Doctrine and Covenants 9:3d) as I studied everything on both sides of the issue and listened to the many voices clamoring for attention.

One day a flash of understanding came to me. I had never dealt with any other scripture the way I was handling this one. Always before I had taken seriously the promise in Alma 16:151 to test the Word by assuming it was true and acting on it. By this method I had developed a strong testimony of the truthfulness and power of many scriptures. Why, then, was I testing this one in the opposite way by assuming it was false until some specific proof was presented to me?

I resolved to change my thinking. I would "experiment on the Word" for a period of time by assuming it was true. I would talk, think, and behave as though ordination for women was God's plan and see what happened.

Several changes occurred almost immediately. I began to experience inner peace where before there had been turmoil and confusion. As I continued to study scripture my eyes were opened to new understandings. Truths that previously had been hidden because of my closed mind were now made plain. Concepts that had not been part of my thinking were given to me by the still, small voice I have come to recognize as God speaking to me. In a variety of ways God began to give me the assurances I needed.

Eventually I reached the point where I was able to say, "Yes, I will accept the ministry of an ordained woman." However, when my own priesthood call was presented just a few weeks later, my struggle began anew. I would be the first ordained woman in my congregation. This would require a much deeper level of commitment than simply to accept someone else's ministry.

My husband Ken was called to the office of priest at the same time I was, and we were ordained during the same service in March 1986. The radically different responses we had point out some of my problems. Ken had anticipated his calling and was making personal, spiritual preparations. He was not surprised in the least. But I had been fighting the thought of a call for months. Deep within me I knew it was coming, yet I couldn't face it.

When the elders came to share what they thought

was good news, Ken readily accepted his call. I cried the entire time they were there. I didn't want to accept their message and was disappointed they didn't share any specific, spiritual "evidence." Before I could accept I needed personal, strong confirmation that this was the Lord's will. I had never seen myself as a risk taker or a person in the forefront. I shrank from this responsibility and began the soul-searching battle all over again.

In my anguish I cried out to God for many nights. "Give me a sign," I demanded. And the answer came, in part, with the following message: "Your confirmation will come in service and in mighty prayer. I love you. You must dwell in that understanding. I will always be right beside you to counsel. Learn increasingly to listen to my voice and shut out all others. Go forward in faith. Knowledge will come. You will not receive the personal validation you seek until you accept and begin to serve. My Spirit has nurtured you and prepared you for this day. Go forth as an act of faith."

With that understanding I reached a turning point. I remembered that part of my commitment to the Lord was in not saying no to any call God had for my life. If this was genuine divine direction, how could I now say no?

When I called my pastor to give my assent, he shared his own experience of confirming evidence which came in the form of a spiritual dream. There was no doubt in his mind that this was God's will. My former pastor also bore his testimony. He had been given evidence of my call in 1983 when Ken was ordained a deacon, but there was no official way to process it then. He spoke of the nature of my ministry and was helpful in giving specific direction.

Ken moved into service willingly after his ordination. I held back, not wanting to hurt some of my friends for whom women's ordination was not acceptable. It was necessary for the Lord to speak to me directly with the understanding, "The time to wait for these friends is past. You have a responsibility now to serve those who voted support for your calling and are expectantly waiting for the blessings of ministry you will bring them."

I have found general acceptance of my ministry from local church members. There are also those who did not accept my call and have absented themselves from local worship services on various occasions. My heart and love are with them because I believe they are responding with spiritual integrity to what they believe is God's will. I also believe that God honors their decision and somehow will show them a way to continue faithful service.

My ministry seems to have brought feelings of increased personal worth to other women. One said to me, "I have always taken Communion from a man. While it has been a good experience, it carried the subtle message, 'You can never be as spiritual as I am or as close to God, simply because you are female.' Now, in taking Communion from a woman I affirm for myself that I am a true, spiritual partner and companion with men. I do not need an intermediary to bring me to God. My femaleness is not a spiritual handicap but a unique asset. I am challenged to nurture my gifts in ways which will allow me to stand in the presence of God as his loving child and servant. I, too, have a calling. I am free now to explore its possibilities. My nature as a woman is part of that calling, and I rejoice in it."

Margaret Athey
Overland Park, Kansas

I have *always* believed that *all* are called according to their gifts. I have never believed that God loved women less than men. Men and women are equal persons in the sight of God who is no respecter of persons; what God would do for one, God would do for another. But, even while I have truly believed all of this, at the same time I have been an accepting person. It has never been my style to offer serious questions as to *why* things are done in such and such a way. That aspect of my personality was especially true in regard to the church. I accepted everything that the church did, and I offered little or no question as to right or wrong.

Whenever I would hear talk about the ordination of women, I chose to ignore it. I felt that if it ever happened, that would be okay and if it didn't, that would be okay, too. In time, I came to know of some women who greatly desired to hold priesthood. I never did.

I had a multitude of opportunities to serve the church. I was richly blessed in my ministry teaching, singing, conducting choirs, directing worship, and the like. I felt fulfilled and deeply satisfied in my church service. The possibility of priesthood for myself was dismissed quickly with the thought that I certainly had enough to do already and would not have time for more.

Two or three times, unexplainable things have happened that have brought strength and enlightenment. One such incident occurred about ten years ago during a stake conference after leading the choir in singing "The Spirit of God Like a Fire Is Burning." The music had been wonderful with the organ, trumpets, and descant. We had worked hard to prepare it. I also had worked with the presider to prepare the order of worship. As I sat there with my heart still pounding from the thrill of the music, it seemed that I was caught up into a vacuum—sort of a tunnel—and I heard the voice of the Lord say, "Margaret, I want more of you."

I didn't hesitate to answer, "My Lord, you know that I don't have more time! Why, I already go to church four nights a week and several hours on Sunday. I have a lot of responsibilities in my congregation, and I try to do them faithfully. Plus, I teach school *every* day and have a husband and three growing children who keep me busy, not to mention several professional and community things!"

When I recall this experience, I marvel that the Lord didn't dismiss me right then for being such an excuse maker. Nor can I imagine that I would "talk back" to God! But God "spoke" to me again (I never "saw" anything and the people near me were not aware of my encounter), "Margaret, I don't want more of your time, I want more of *you*."

That incident took no time at all. But it happened. I was so completely wrapped in the love of God that tears poured down my face. I didn't understand the incident. I only knew that something powerful—something beyond myself—had happened to me.

That incident did not change my life. But it made a deep impression. It revealed to me that God was personally interested in me. And, for my part, I decided to respond by throwing myself into my work with greater intensity. I cherished the experience. It was only recently that I have connected that experience with my priesthood call.

I have learned that priesthood is more than officiating at the sacraments and ordinances. It means offering spiritual guidance, ministering with the power of God wherever and whenever the need arises. Priesthood is offering leadership to the people of the church. Since my ordination I have been privileged many times to do all of these things: offer spiritual guidance to a friend, witness with the power of God in my Sunday school class, and offer sound leadership to a church committee or study group. This is ordinary-type stuff, yet endowed with a new dimension that leaves me humbled and grateful.

Women are not called to do what men have always done—certainly not to replace them. Women have unique gifts that many men do not hold as strengths. It is our unique strengths that we are called to offer. We are not to compete with men, but to supplement the ministries of the church by offering ministries that have been missing—nurturing, supporting, giving attention to detail. I walk in places unique to me. Those are the places I am called to serve.

Anita Ruth Bates
Edgerton, Alberta, Canada

On the day of my ordination as a deacon, I experienced an awakening of the Lord's Spirit within me which truly enveloped my whole body and gave me a more perfect peace than anything I had known before.

Several important life experiences and events from early in my life tempered me gradually into the steady service of the Lord. I did not, however, always take heed to the push of the Lord's Spirit to serve and walk with the Lord. There have been tests, trials, and tribulations for which, periodically, I have suffered greatly.

In 1977 when my father became seriously ill, I quit my working professions in accounting and semi-truck driving to come home and take care of my parents. Before he passed away that year, my father shared with me that someday women would be called to the priesthood in the RLDS Church. He also advised me to prepare accordingly as I would be called to the priesthood to "serve and walk with God."

There were many opportunities in the ensuing years for me to grow. In two years I took the leadership for the Ribstone vacation church school. Then I accepted the leadership of the women's department. I visited Australia, and in the main branch of the church in Sydney I witnessed such unity of the Lord's Spirit and love portrayed by the Australian Saints that it gave me renewed vigor, inspiration, and faith to continue to serve the Lord according to my gifts. My patriarchal blessing cautioned me to be on a constant watch for intervention of evil, and it also affirmed that I would be called to serve in the Lord's ministry.

A special experience of ministry came when I represented our branch in an ecumenical service and shared with ministers of other churches. I was nervous, but as I offered a silent prayer asking for wisdom, calmness, and quietness of spirit to deliver my sermon, I felt the Spirit flow through me. As I took my turn to speak, I viewed several RLDS members in the congregation. It was as if a light was beaming from them to me, bringing further calmness, support, and love. Many people, representing various denominations, came to me afterward to express their joy, love, and support.

Teaching a priesthood class has been another rewarding experience. I was overjoyed and delighted as I prepared each class session. This was a uniting, sharing experience with the other priesthood members of the Ribstone Branch.

I have been fortunate to experience the guidance and direction of the Lord's Spirit and to have the ministry of encouragement administered to me by numerous members of my family and the extended family of our congregation. All have been Christlike in recognizing my God-given abilities and have encouraged me to move ahead with full support.

Floy L. Bennett
Independence, Missouri

At the Santa Fe Stake conference in September 1985, I was one of four women presented for ordination. I had been called to the office of elder.

We four women were among the first in the church to have calls presented. We were also the first to be rejected. The following night I could not sleep. The occasion had produced some trauma for me and I felt an overwhelming loneliness.

During the night it began to rain. These are God's tears, I thought. How many times have we brought him grief by our unwillingness to let him speak to our hearts? Jesus knew sorrow for "he was despised, rejected, a man of sorrows and acquainted with grief." The rain continued to fall, and I wept also, knowing I was not alone and that eventually God's will would be done.

Our names were presented again, along with others, the following February. This time they were approved by the stake conference.

Long before the presentation of Section 156 I had growing feelings about the need for women to share their gifts more fully in the church's mission. For a year and a half during the 1970s, I wrote weekly articles for the back page of our church bulletin at the Ridgewood Congregation. One part was a series on the importance of growth as exemplified by little children. I often felt God's guiding Spirit as I tried to put on paper what I was not allowed to say behind the pulpit.

In February 1985, prior to my priesthood call, I was the last of several speakers at church to give a report on our congregational retreat. In my attempt to give needed ministry that day, the Lord opened the heavens, and I was enveloped by the power of the Holy Spirit. Our retreat theme had been forgiveness, and as I spoke the beauty of a forgiving spirit was brought home to us. The Lord's presence was so obvious that tears washed the faces of many. They expressed to me later their recognition and appreciation for the beauty of God's loving presence in our service that morning.

This is one event that helped to prepare me for my call and ordination. I knew the Lord could use me in ways that I would not have believed possible a few years earlier. Because this opportunity came late in my life, it bothered me. But I remembered that God takes what we have, even in our later years, and makes it enough to meet the needs of those who look to us for ministry. My years have never been idle years; God has just opened the gate to a larger field of service.

I can see more clearly that there is a place for women in a ministry that is special because we are women. A telephone call late one night asking me to come and administer to a young woman who was in great distress is a case in point. When I said I would come and bring my husband with me, I was told that I should not bring him. The woman had been abused and would not allow a man to touch her. Because no other ordained woman was available, I went alone. That night I was made aware of another good reason for women in the priesthood. There are places where men cannot go or are not acceptable. No doubt the reverse is true also.

Another occasion of God's intervention occurred in a time of my own deep distress. I had entered a hospital for what was considered minor surgery. Everything seemed to go well, so in four days I was sent home. The following day I developed complications and had to be readmitted. I was told that I would have to have medication intravenously around the clock for six days. What a blow! I was missing my Temple School classes, and here I lay helpless and discouraged. I tried to pray but could not communicate with the Lord. Oh, I could say words, but I could not relate to or feel God's presence. My mind was on my pain and my helpless state. I cried and indulged in a lot of self-pity, feeling abandoned and alone.

Early the next morning, a member of the hospital staff came into the room I shared with another patient. I sensed immediately why she had come. My roommate, Barbara, was told that her illness was terminal and far advanced. When the staff person left the room I heard Barbara crying—great, wracking sobs that tore at my heart. I looked at myself lying prone—various tubes attached to my tortured body—and wondered how I could help my suffering roommate. Slowly, I removed the sheet that covered me. With difficulty I scooted my legs to the edge of the bed and raised my body to an erect position. With my feet on the floor, I gathered the paraphernalia that encumbered me and pushed it ahead of me until I reached the foot of Barbara's bed. I touched her feet and said, "Barbara, I am a minister, may I pray for you?" She opened her eyes in surprise, looked at me for a moment, and then nodded her head.

As I started to pray, the clouds that had encompassed me for days dispersed and an overwhelming sense of peace came over both of us. I felt God was not only standing with me and supporting me in my effort to be an instrument of peace and comfort to this woman whom I did not know, but Christ was *in* me. My cup was full to overflowing. Barbara and I were both God's children, sisters in this exciting enterprise we call life.

My concept of the scope of ministry is constantly being enlarged. It encompasses every area of life and may be given by any person, ordained or unordained, who has compassion and love for God's children, everywhere and in whatever situation—in the home, neighborhood, church, and the whole wide world. A desire to minister gives motivation and impetus to learn the skills for ministry. And there is always more to learn.

Jean (Hawkins) Broadaway
Nuneaton, Warwickshire, England

Priesthood ministry has always been important to me as a member of the Reorganized Church of Jesus Christ of Latter Day Saints. Here was a church different from any I had known with regard to the calling of the ordained. Many times I have sensed the sacredness and rightness of the act as calls have been brought before the body of people for their approval. On occasion I have wanted to stand in respect of the authority represented as ministers have mounted the rostrum for worship.

Even after speculation began some years ago regarding ordaining women, there was no way I could envision a change in priesthood structure—nor did I want a change. After all, there were many ways that women could serve if they so desired. My life had certainly been guided and stretched with each new task the Lord presented to me, and I was in many ways fulfilled. I could not comprehend any woman—much less myself—wanting the responsibility of a priesthood call.

Prior to the 1984 World Conference Seventy Huw Evans arranged a tour from the British Isles to include Conference week in Independence, Missouri. Along with fifty others, I traveled to America. Many of us were to serve as delegates. I remember so clearly sitting in the Auditorium conference chamber while the inspired document was read. The Spirit was abundantly evident; there seemed to be an almost unreal stillness. Although the room was full of people, I was alone with my God and my beliefs. Without a shadow of a doubt, I knew this was God's will. But how could I relate this experience to others, especially after all I had said on previous occasions against the issue?

Upon our return to the British Isles, I attended a regional women's weekend at Dunfield House Conference Centre. Those of us who had served as World Conference delegates were asked to share our testimonies. With the exception of one sister, each of us stood to bear an affirmative testimony—all remarkably similar even though we had not had a chance to share our thoughts with one another since our return from the United States. I am convinced our tour group of fifty Saints was led to go to that World Conference so that we could return with the joy of sharing the good news of a prophetic church.

Life continued much the same for me. Yet in some strange way women's ministries took on new meaning. I was sure it would be several years before we saw the ordination of women in the British Isles. However, over the following months I was occasionally prompted by the Holy Spirit to prepare myself for added responsibility. At times this would come during the night; sometimes during a worship service I felt the same "need."

One Friday evening my district president called at my home. He said very little and stayed just a few moments. As he left I wondered why he had come—it seemed so pointless. A short time afterwards my pastor telephoned to invite me to his home. As I drove my car out of the garage that night I knew why. "Please Lord, don't let it be me," I prayed as I drove. The district president was also there as I was told of my call to the office of priest. The same feeling of aloneness came over me that I had witnessed during World Conference. I knew my calling was from the Lord, and I trembled as I looked into the face of my pastor, a young man who I had watched develop and grow over the years. I respected his integrity and was aware of his courage in processing my call.

Upon returning home, I spent the whole night in prayer, shedding many tears. The burden of responsibility seemed so great I felt ill for the next few weeks. I turned to my patriarchal blessing for counsel, and a portion of it leapt out from the page: "How fortunate we are that we can share the blessings that come to us as a result of his church through which we enjoy the blessings of the restoration of the priesthood. As you continue to meditate upon this it will become a deep and abiding testimony of the divinity of his church."

I made my decision to accept the call, and along with two young men presented myself to our local congregation. Many of the women offered their prayers of support, as did our younger priesthood members. But the people who I expected to talk with me and share their thoughts—the same ones who had encouraged me over the years—made no mention of my call at all. I was terribly hurt. After the call was accepted by a majority of the people at the Central England District conference, many people telephoned to share their testimonies of my calling. Some expressed that it was made known to them under the influence of the Spirit while we were in America.

I remember clearly one phrase from the ordination prayer in December 1985: "Be sure, Jean, that this calling that you have accepted comes from your heavenly Father, and even that you have been marked from birth for this calling to his priesthood." It was a joy that day to look out at the sea of faces before me. There were my family members whose love and support has always been a firm foundation in my life, my church family who nurtured me over the years, my neighbors and friends who respected the witness the church has to offer, and even those church members who originally found my ordination difficult to accept.

The first few weeks following my ordination were tense. There were many things to learn, and I wanted it to be so right. I was apprehensive the first time I served the Lord's Supper, certain everyone would hear the glasses clinking together. But the sincerity and devotion of the Saints were much in evidence as I moved along the rows. The realization has come to me that I have been called because of my gifts which I should offer in service—not called simply to become like my fellow ministers.

I am blessed that I enjoy all aspects of the office of priest. Family visiting is always a joy. I relate well to the elderly and have shared many wonderful moments with children. I enjoy preparing for preaching, finding it wonderful to dwell upon a scripture and to see the different ways it can relate to a congregation of people.

Since my ordination it has been good to see many other women in the British Isles taking their places in ministry. I see this as a natural expression of ministry as "servanthood"; God, after all, is no respecter of persons and uses both men and women together to meet the needs of humanity. I will continue with God's help to find new ways to respond so that the needs of others might be met.

Denise Marie (Campbell) Buscavage
Baker, Florida

I knew it was coming. Everyone was talking about it. We discussed it with fellow church members at Wednesday evening prayer services, at socials, and with our closest friends in our homes. It seemed like almost every conversation in some way or another managed to include discussion of women being called to the priesthood.

Everyone with whom I spoke seemed to have accepted the idea of women in the priesthood. Coming from a background of church members so active and supportive and having been active in numerous congregations, I too felt that I should be able to support Section 156. But I wasn't. It's just not right to have women in the priesthood.

Because everyone else was so accepting, I didn't share my true feelings. If I didn't think about it, maybe it wouldn't come about. But it did. When we heard the news from World Conference in April 1984, I was quite upset. Over the summer I shared my feelings with my husband. We had many discussions, and I shed many tears. Although he listened, I didn't feel he gave me the support I needed. I found out later that he, too, had had some of the same feelings I had. But because of his own priesthood call to elder and selection as counselor to the district president, he felt obligated to fully support and implement church policies and revelations.

Because my whole life centered around the church, I felt I had no choice but to accept all this. I would never leave the church; that was not an option. As I struggled and prayed, I decided to rely on God. I would stop fighting it, accept it, and go from there. God had always taken care of things in the past, and I had no reason to believe God would desert me now. Only a few women would be called anyway, I reasoned, and they would be from Independence or from some other district than mine. It wouldn't influence me directly, and I could live with that.

Then the calls came to the Pensacola District for six women, thirty-five to fifty miles away. That was getting a little close, and I knew each of the women. They were such loving, beautiful, caring people. If that's the kind of people God was going to call, then I could continue in faith knowing God would help me in my acceptance of those calls.

Then it happened in our congregation. At the beginning of the service one Sunday morning, our pastor gave the names of several with priesthood calls; the last one was a woman. I was stunned. It almost took my breath away. As I sat there and cried, no one seemed to notice me. Perhaps they thought I had been touched by the service. Afterward, everyone congratulated her. I watched from a distance and left the church with tears streaming down my face. How could this be happening in my own congregation?

The struggles I felt I had resolved returned. Again, no one else seemed to be having a problem. I felt all alone in my confusion. How could I ever raise my hand in support of this call?

A week prior to the business meeting to support the new priesthood calls, the pastor asked me to give the invocation at the business meeting. Although I didn't want to, I said I would. Then I was faced with trying to work out my attitude. I prayed and agonized over it the whole week. When I was still in tears on Saturday afternoon, my husband offered to pray with me about it. Although I felt somewhat better, I still did not have the confirmation I needed.

I was still unsure and anxious as we started the service by singing, "The Spirit of God Like a Fire Is Burning." By the completion of the hymn I truly felt the Spirit of God burning within me. I finally had the assurance of this woman's calling. I was able to give the invocation and later was able to share my testimony concerning my struggles with Section 156 and to support this priesthood call.

My own priesthood call came in April 1986. While at the reunion grounds for our branch retreat, my husband and brother-in-law asked me to walk down to the lake with them. I knew what was coming.

I had been actively involved with Calling and Caring ministry in my congregation and was visiting several families in their homes. I enjoyed doing it, and it felt comfortable. Even so, I felt humble and unworthy as I received the news of my call. Why me when there were so many devoted ladies in our branch so much more deserving? Yet it felt good to me.

All my life I had been searching for a way to serve God and others. I had finally found it through Calling and Caring ministry. Visiting in the homes was what I enjoyed doing. Now God confirmed this by my call to the office of teacher. I had no great spiritual experience confirming my call. I again trusted God to lead me as I have been led in the past.

As an ordained teacher, I have continued to visit and share in the homes. I feel my calling is to my home congregation, my family members, my students at school, and to my fellow coworkers. God is directing and guiding my life. I pray daily for God's discerning Spirit and desire always to be found doing the divine will.

Vivian Collins Campbell
Tulsa, Oklahoma

Ever since 1970, when I was asked occasionally what I thought about women in the priesthood, I stated that I thought the constraints upon women were cultural, not divine. However, I worked for change more by evolution than revolution. I stated that I probably would not see women in the priesthood during my lifetime. I felt sorrow about this because of the great need for more human resources in the church while, at the same time, resources of many women were being underutilized, ignored, or wasted.

In December 1983 my husband, Glen, was bishop for the Northern Plains and Prairie Provinces Region. Our home was in Great Falls, Montana. I was completing a doctoral program in Michigan with Glen's encouragement. This educational program was pursued because of promptings by the Holy Spirit to prepare myself in specific ways for further service in the church. As the time came in December for my doctoral defense, I prayed one night that I would become aware of how I could most effectively give my life in service when the program was complete.

This prayer was answered by an experience that I feel was a divine encounter. I awoke from a refreshing sleep—which for me was unusual—with three clear, firm convictions: (1) I needed to prepare myself for priesthood responsibility; (2) I would be called upon to suffer; and (3) if I would always remember to focus on the Christ I would have strength and courage that would be required and the suffering would not be more than I could stand.

As I reflected upon the meaning of this experience I thought, The church is not ready for women to accept priesthood responsibility. It must mean that my call is to serve in priesthood capacity after death. For quite some time I had been experiencing constant, excruciating physical pain. Thinking about the possibility of death coming soon was not altogether unpleasant but in some ways a sweet relief. Although I would not choose to die, I was willing. I assumed that this was what was meant by the suffering that I would need to endure. However, I remembered the promise that if I would always focus on the Christ, I would have the strength and courage that would be required.

When I finished in Michigan and returned to Montana, I told no one of the experience. I knew that the possibility that I might die soon would bring sorrow to my spouse, and I didn't want to cause him unnecessary grief in case my interpretation was wrong. I then organized all my personal files to make retrieval easy for him and in general set everything in order. I vowed to share with Glen when I felt more sure.

One week before the 1984 World Conference, I found out about a treatment that had good possibilities of relieving my pain. I told the doctor that I needed to think about it awhile before deciding to be treated. I thought privately that if I did not live long, it would be a big waste of the church's money.

I cannot adequately describe the profound joy and personal relief I experienced upon hearing the first reading of what is now Section 156. All around me in the conference chamber I could see persons who were shocked and in disbelief. I felt compassion for them, but at the same time I felt an overwhelming excitement about what this could mean for the corporate life of the church.

As I reinterpreted my December 1983 experience, I thought that perhaps I would be called in the near future. As I reflected about being called upon to suffer, I supposed it meant that as a pioneer there would be times of suffering due to those unwilling to accept my ministry.

My call was initiated by Western Montana's district president in December 1985. He had a personal testimony that my call must not wait any longer; therefore, he presented it even though he knew the Great Falls pastor was not fully supportive. The pastor made it clear when presenting it to the congregation that he did not initiate it. He did not permit me to speak of my acceptance but just presented my name for a vote. In spite of this, the majority voted in favor. A few people who voted on the negative side assured me later that it had nothing to do with me personally; it was because I was a woman. I accepted their responses with smiles but found it amusing to think that, to me, being a woman *is* fairly personal!

I enjoyed increasing responsibilities during my first year as an elder. My first three sermons were during a three-week period at three different reunions in Alaska, Alberta, and Montana on three different topics. After our transfer to Tulsa Stake, I was ordained a high priest in May 1988.

I have come to understand more fully what is meant by being called upon to suffer. The treatment to alleviate my physical suffering has been successfully completed. Because I no longer experience great pain, I have more energy to devote to ministry. The suffering I experience now from time to time is not for me personally but is on behalf of the church. I don't fully understand this yet, but my understanding is growing. I am confident that if I always remember to focus on the Christ, I will have the strength and courage required.

Ethel (Boswell) Carlile
St. Joseph, Missouri

I was at the 1984 World Conference and vividly recall my feelings as I heard the document read. The sequence of my thinking was this: (1) Isn't this wonderful? It is so right; (2) I wasn't expecting it to come at this Conference; and (3) I'm glad my age will exempt me.

A lady sitting a few seats from me asked at the close of the delegates' and visitors' briefing, "Well, what do you think of this?" My response was that I was pleased and felt it was right. Then she wanted to know why I felt so.

I was rather surprised to be so bluntly challenged, but I'm certain that an experience in a women's class at Warsaw, Missouri (our home at that time), had prepared me. So I answered by quoting words found both in the Bible and the Book of Mormon, that in the sight of God there is no bond or free, black or white, Jew or Gentile, male or female.

The woman said she had never thought of that, but she had reservations of her own. Perhaps I might have had some also, had I not had the experience mentioned before. In our women's class, one sister declared that she was *certain* our church would never ordain women. The Good Spirit bore witness right at that moment that such a judgment was not right, and the scripture just quoted came to mind as verification of God's impartiality.

I have to smile at my own thinking that my age would exempt me! Since my ordination as an elder, I see that in God's sight neither sex, life's station, *nor* age are points of prejudice. In fact, I am grateful to have this new challenge and opportunity to serve come in my late sixties. My four children are grown, and I now have the time to study and prepare which I would not have had, had my call come earlier in life.

The first indication of my call came in late December 1985. I had a dream in which I was preaching to a congregation. As I awoke I reflected on it. One factor was that the congregation was one of the most vocal against Section 156. Another factor was my attitude toward dreams. In the past, I had felt that many people used dreams as an all-too-frequent substitution of what that person had already deemed he or she wanted—and the dream would verify it!

Interesting! I was being shown another way in which I must not limit God, neither by age nor by means of communication. This has been a growing conceptual influence.

For the next six months, I felt a restlessness, an urgency, that I had never experienced before. In early May 1986 I wrote a note which I entitled, "For Future Reference." In it was expressed a feeling of a possible call. Also, I noted the office to which I felt I might be called.

The next Sunday, our pastor asked if he could visit our home that afternoon. At the appointed hour he and the stake president knocked at our door. The instant I saw them I *knew* why they had come. I had never mentioned any of my feelings to my husband. I felt these experiences must be between me and the Lord. (Anyway, I knew Jack would be happy and this might color my thinking.)

They promptly stated the purpose of their visit and asked me if I had any evidence of a call. How glad I was that I had written my "future reference" note. It was truly a strength and testimony to each of us.

June 29, 1986, was a significant date for me. It was my husband's sixty-eighth birthday and our forty-fifth wedding anniversary. It was also the day my priesthood call was approved!

From the beginning, Jack, who is also an elder, was truly elated as he envisioned our being able to minister together. My greatest joy has come by serving at his side. I have drawn strength, comfort, and unflagging support from him, and I realize I have been singularly blessed by having his support. He has shown nothing but pride in my accomplishments, and his encouragement is a constant blessing.

I have participated many times in the ordinance of administration, and several have had significant impact on me. One time my husband and I were called to the bedside of a brother who had struggled with the call of women to the priesthood. The warm feeling of fraternity that we experienced was indeed rewarding.

I'm not certain which activities in the last decade or so can be said to have been contributing factors for this call to priesthood. Like Nephi, I was born of "goodly parents" and their influence has always been a guiding factor in my life. Opportunities have been abundant to serve throughout my lifetime. At sixteen, I was asked to teach a class of eleven-year-old boys that the pastor and several others had given up on. Since then I have taught all ages, from nursery to adults. I've been a women's leader for several congregations and Central Missouri Stake. I have been a worship chairman, music director, reunion class instructor, prebaptismal teacher, and helped in cottage meetings.

I have always tried to make myself available, many

times taking jobs I felt ill-qualified for when no one else would do them. I have found that being plunged in over my head has caused me to lean upon God who is always available to help.

I am grateful for the opportunities that I am being given to serve. To be ordained and never be given the opportunity to serve would have been disappointing. As we serve, we grow by disciplined study, prayer, and dedication. To this end, I lend all that I now am or ever hope to become.

Mary Jane Carter
Pueblo, Colorado

In the spring of 1984, my husband was preparing to teach a series of classes on upcoming World Conference resolutions. As a prelude to those classes, I suggested I teach a class on revelation. Preparing for it, I remembered the advice of Dr. Roy Cheville. He said that rather than running back to Conference with, "What did the Lord say? Is there a new revelation?" participants ought to take a look at the world and ask, "Where do we see that the world has need? What problems do we have on which the Lord could shed new light and understanding?"

Some weeks later I sat in the Auditorium conference chamber and heard the words, "The temple shall be dedicated to the pursuit of peace. It shall be for reconciliation and for healing of the spirit.... By its ministries an attitude of wholeness of body, mind, and spirit as a desirable end toward which to strive will be fostered." I remembered my own experience of several weeks before and was thrilled and humbled to hear the words of instruction regarding the building of the Temple.

When that portion concerning the ordination of women was read my only comment was, "Well, good! Now those women who feel they have a call can be ordained." I was glad that *those* women could now give expression to their special gifts and talents in a unique way through ordination; however, that was quite remote from my own needs and desires.

On the day the document was approved, my husband and I dashed out to dinner, then returned to the Auditorium where the service was already in progress. We slipped into the back row, and, moved by the day's events, I lifted my heart up to my Lord in thanksgiving.

"O Lord, I would do anything for you," I silently prayed. "I would scrub the floors of the Temple, I would wash the windows...."

"Would you be ordained?" God asked.

"Would I what?"

"Would you be ordained?"

Surprised, overwhelmed—ordination was not exactly what I had in mind. I don't know how long I sat there before answering, "Yes, I would." But then I added, "If you are calling me to be ordained, there must be some confirmation of office." I went through each of the offices. Nothing. I breathed a sigh of relief. I certainly must have misunderstood the experience that had just transpired. Unbelieving, I asked for confirmation of the experience. Once again I said, "O Lord, I would do anything for you. I would scrub the floors of the Temple, I would wash the windows...."

"Would you be ordained?"

"Would I what?"

"Would you be ordained?"

Again I asked for confirmation of the office and went through each priesthood office. Still, no confirmation came. But as I reviewed my own giftedness, I knew the Lord was not asking me to be something I wasn't. God was calling me to use and further develop my talents, gifts, and abilities in ways that would bring ministry.

After retiring that night, I reflected on the day's events. Still doubting the event that had transpired, I once again asked for confirmation of the task to which I had been called. The experience was repeated exactly as it had occurred earlier.

I returned home from Conference and began to study and prepare for the work to which I knew the Lord had called me. I read the *Priesthood Manual* and enrolled in all the Temple School courses that were offered in my district. The first Temple School class I enrolled in was entitled, "The Office of Elder." As I took my place in the class, a kind, well-meaning gentleman approached and said, "The classes for the women are downstairs." I just smiled and assured him I had come to take this one.

The official notification of my call as an elder came in September 1985 from my husband, who was the pastor. I did not give him an immediate response; however, I hesitated only a few hours. I determined the Lord had called and I chose to follow, even if I had to stand by myself.

My affirmative response brought with it a buoyancy of spirit such as I had never known. That buoyancy lasted about three days. Then I found myself back on earth. "Mary Jane, whatever have you got yourself into?" I asked. There was never any doubt of the Lord's call. There was only a sense of being overwhelmed by the responsibility I was accepting. Next day I was back on cloud nine. I went through that kind of emotional roller coaster until the day of my ordination.

Since that day I have known great joy. I have been upheld by warm, loving acceptance in my congregation, district, and in the setting of the World Conference. During Conference, as we stood in line waiting to go into the conference chamber to serve Communion, a young black man came by, and touching me on the shoulder said, "I so appreciate what you're doing." Apostle Paul's familiar scripture took on new meaning. (I sensed that young man was saying, "If the church can fully accept women, maybe there is still hope for us.")

In August 1986 I traveled to Salt Lake City to speak to the Sunstone Society. The topic for discussion was "Women in the Priesthood," and the panel included Paul Edwards, Temple School director, and Dana Cochrane-Wiley, a young woman who was ordained a teacher in the Salt Lake City Branch. When each of us had borne our testimony and the meeting was opened to audience participation, one young woman said, "Last January I wrote an article for one of our publications. Following its distribution I was asked if I desired priesthood in the Mormon church. I assured those who asked I did not. However, I think that after listening to your presentation today, I have been persuaded. I think you have changed my mind."

When all the rhetoric has died, when all the debates and theological arguments have been presented and won or lost, when all the scriptures have been quoted to "prove" one view or another, there will remain for me one truth: the Lord called me to be ordained. Had my call never been processed, had the congregation never approved the call, had the district conference turned it down, that one truth would still remain.

Elizabeth (Bettye) Day Cervola
Mobile, Alabama

I was sixty-six years old when my pastor visited me one Sunday afternoon in September 1986 and told me the purpose of his visit. I was called to the office of teacher.

Tears welled up in my eyes and ran down my face. My first words were, "But Larry, I am not worthy." We talked at length, and he assured me that it came to him from God. I was so emotionally overcome that I did not give him an answer. The next day I left on an already-planned, month-long vacation. Uppermost in my mind, however, was my call.

My vacation included a stop at Kirtland Temple where I had never visited before. Yet I had always felt a connection to it because my great-grandmother, Betsy Grace Woodstock, and her family had lived there and had helped build it. I recall the story of how Betsy Grace helped her mother, Samantha Holsbrook Woodstock, break their china for the temple walls. So, my heart was full the day I visited the Temple. I would love to have lingered there alone to be saturated with the good Spirit that I felt.

As we traveled on through the grandeur of God's creation, more and more that still, small voice whispered to me. Peace and joy filled my heart, and I hurried home to let my pastor know that I most humbly accepted my call.

Looking back, I felt that the call to serve God had come at an early age. My grandmother gave me my first Bible when I was eleven. I finished reading it right after age twelve. I always loved to study my

Sunday school lessons and to search the scriptures. It was my childhood desire to be a missionary or a missionary's wife, but it was not to be.

I graduated from Independence Sanitarium and Hospital in 1943. Several years later I married a military career man. For long spans of time our family was cut off from the church. We attended army chapels wherever we were, and for one long stretch of about five years we attended a Methodist church where I served as a Sunday school teacher and director and participated in the women's circles. After retirement, we settled in my home city of Mobile. That was twenty-four years ago. Since then, my husband has died and my three daughters now have their own lives and families, although they all live close by.

I was present in the Auditorium when the inspired document was read for the first time. I must confess that my first reactions were disbelief and rejection. It took a lot of meditation and prayer before I accepted it. During the subsequent services of that Conference I kept my eyes riveted on President Smith and my heart was opened. To me, it narrowed down to one question: Is this the mind and will of God or of man? In the ensuing hours and days, the Spirit bore witness to me of its rightness, and I joyfully stood with the assembly to vote in assent to the document.

I thought how wonderful it would be to be younger and have my lifelong desires fulfilled. I felt the call to ordained ministry would be for younger, more energetic women. Thus, I was surprised and overcome when my pastor visited me on a Sunday afternoon to convey my call in such a gentle, kind, and loving way.

I thought on this during the days and weeks that followed, and though I would have loved for the

Angel Gabriel to visit me and affirm this, nothing like that occurred. It was the still, small voice of God that filled me with the assurance that this is what God wanted for me. When the time came for our branch business meeting, I had no qualms to stand and accept my call.

Since my ordination, I have felt something growing within me. There is a keener desire to serve and study. I have visited our older members, have participated in many services, and have availed myself of every Temple School opportunity. The meaning of the word "ministry" has expanded in my viewpoint. There is a deeper feeling that accompanies the meaning of serving. I am so grateful to God for his Son, for his church, and for the courageous prophet he has given us for this time.

Jeanne M. (Benson) Chase
Independence, Missouri

I was born into a family that belonged to the Reorganized Church of Jesus Christ of Latter Day Saints. They deemed it an honor to serve in the church. We attended services regularly, made our financial accounting, and when I was twelve years old I was asked to help with smaller children in vacation church school and junior church. I played the piano for services and wrote my first story for *Stepping Stones* when I was fourteen.

My husband, Ken, was not a member of the church when we met but joined six months before we married. It has been a tremendous blessing that he recognized the Holy Spirit working in his life and chose to make his commitment to Christ. Soon after he joined the church, he was called to the priesthood and has served as pastor of four congregations in Center Stake.

My role in our church life was fairly traditional. I rejoiced at Ken's opportunities to serve and supported him faithfully. I contributed in the usual ways that women do by teaching church school, vacation church school, girls' programs, singing in choirs, and writing some for church publications. Life was always busy and always changing. There has never been a time when I had lacked opportunities to serve people.

Christ's love and his action in people's lives have always been especially clear to me through children, and when the "new" curriculum was produced by the World Church in the early 1970s, I thrilled at the possibilities in the innovative methods which were introduced. Where I had "saved" creative ideas before, I now spent them freely, knowing there would always be another when I needed it. God blessed me with an optimism I had never experienced before.

I was sitting in the conference chamber in 1984 when I first heard the words, "Do not wonder that some women are being called...." I felt then that there was a possibility that I would be called. I did not want to think about it, though, and I was able to consider priesthood calls for women as priesthood calls for *other* women. I was joyful and uplifted at God's new gift to the church.

As time passed, the thought came to me that I might eventually be called, but I deliberately set the thought aside. That worked quite well for a time, but the impression came more and more frequently. Sometimes I could go for a week without thinking about "being a priesthood member."

The assurance that I was being called of God grew stronger; I no longer could avoid thinking about it. At the same time, I, who have always been active in church, began to feel a rather different kind of caring for my brothers and sisters. There were many times when people seemed to respond openly to my ministry. Several times when I was teaching children, I saw adults in the room listening intently, and I knew I was teaching them, too.

The agitation of the Holy Spirit affected everything I did. It was always with me. It gave me energy, it gave me creativity, its intrusion often annoyed me, but I could not push it away. I knew I was called.

I was so sure of my calling that I thought it must be in process by the Center Stake High Council of which my husband is a member. That procedure is confidential, and I did not want to cause Ken any awkwardness by telling him what I already knew. From time to time a comment would burst out, and I would immediately wish it hadn't. It was difficult for us at that time; both of us wanted to talk yet neither one could.

I felt very much alone, but I was alone with my God—and that's not a bad place to be. Out of my aloneness came the understanding that the service of any person may not be compared with the service of another. Jesus Christ is the only standard. That realization gave me the courage I needed. It overcame my difficulty in trying to see myself as I had viewed men serving God's people. I knew there was a place for me in God's "field of white harvest."

I had a desire to know the office to which I was called. One day as I was reading, I came across a description of an elder (not the passage in the Doctrine and Covenants), and I felt I was reading a description of myself. Later, I tried to find it but I could not. I do not even know from what book I read, but I knew I was called to serve God's people as an elder.

Soon after that, Ken and I were in the kitchen and with my back to him I said, "Don't look at me and don't answer. I know I have a call to the office of elder." He said nothing, and we finished our work in quiet. Just voicing that to him relieved some of the pressure I was experiencing.

Ken told me afterward that at the next meeting of the high council, when my call was approved, he said to my pastor, "Will you please tell her soon? She knows she is called. She knows the office, and it is as if we've had an elephant in the living room that we couldn't talk about."

My pastor and his counselor told me about my call

just before prayer service the next Wednesday evening. My husband was there with me, and my reply was, "Finally, we can talk about it!"

I accepted the call and was one of the first women ordained at Stone Church. Since then I have been ordained a high priest and set apart to the Center Stake High Council. A number of people who are unable to accept the priesthood ministry of women have left Stone Church. The ones who remain, for the most part, have been very supportive of women. Many go out of their way to make positive comments to me, and when I serve Communion, women are particularly outgoing, smiling, thanking me, patting my hand, whispering "God bless you."

In addition to rostrum ministry, committee work, and visiting, much of my ministry is in response to requests for administration. These requests come from men and women, ordained and unordained, of various ages. Because of the number of people who have sought my ministry and who began to seek it soon after my ordination, I realize that there has been a substantial base of acceptance of and desire for women in priesthood ministry even before it became available.

More and more people are accepting the fact that an ordained woman is not an ordained man. Her words, her mannerisms, and her thinking are just a few of the differences. While there are people in favor of women's ministry and people opposed to women's ministry, I believe there is a congregation of good people who are waiting to see how it will work, waiting to see the "Word made flesh."

I thank my Lord for that gift of "agitation" by the Holy Spirit, for revealing his will to me, and for offering me a place to serve among his people.

Carley J. (Knisley) Cole
Didsbury, Alberta, Canada

I had quietly resolved the issue of women's ordination a year or more before the 1984 World Conference. Except for tradition, there seemed no justifiable reason for treating women different from men with regard to priesthood. I was willing to respect that tradition but suspected the time was approaching for a move beyond those cultural bounds. So, in one sense, I wasn't surprised as the document was read to the 1984 World Conference. However, I was surprised at the depth of my emotional response. First, there was an overwhelming sense of worth; then there was a fearful sense of possible responsibility.

The sense of worth was surprising because I thought I knew that priesthood are of no greater worth in God's eyes than others; they merely have special responsibilities. But somehow a message of inferiority had penetrated my subconscious. When the document was read I was nearly overcome by the validation of my—and my sisters'—worth in the eyes of our creator. Obviously, we don't need to be ordained to have this affirmed, but as females we no longer need feel excluded because of some predestined subclassification or inherent incapability.

I suspect this was being experienced by other women present at that hour. A humbling and joyous glow allowed me to remain unthreatened as I listened to the voices of opposition which quickly followed. Even if the document had failed to pass, that moment in time could not have been taken from me!

The second feeling—apprehension—followed quickly and caused considerable soul-searching. Ordination could happen to *me*! How could I know if a call would be "of God" or just a human assumption because my giftedness happens to have more exposure than that of some quiet woman who is really the backbone of nurturing and caring? If no call came, would I feel disappointment or relief? How would I deal with the responsibility? I've always been "handed" assignments and had the priesthood to act as a buffer. If called I would lose the comfort my current role afforded that didn't include the hassle and responsibility of being "on call" to minister. And perhaps most discomforting, how would I react to a sister who experiences the disappointment of not receiving a call?

To protect and prepare myself, I began an internal dialogue of possibilities, a game of self-preservation I learned to play years ago. I remembered some "awesome" assignments I had received in times past which I'd survived. So, with the support of God and others, I'd likely survive ordination. If I weren't called, I reminded myself of the tremendous importance of the call to membership. All giftedness is not necessarily best expressed or developed in priesthood.

But the call to the office of priest did come. I wasn't surprised. Indeed, I had had a growing sense of restlessness regarding a call. My surprises were to come *after* my ordination, first of all as a faith crisis.

Somehow I had anticipated that my faith and confidence would increase, perhaps now as an "authority" on divine matters. That was scary. Inside myself I knew I had "clay feet" like everyone else and was most certainly not infallible! Although I had been a student of scripture, church history, "all good books," leadership courses, and worship/drama workshops, I still felt inadequate. Delivering a sermon was fun, but in preparation there came a growing fear that I might state or infer some theological untruth. I was uncomfortable with the prospect of one-on-one counseling encounters. I had a sense of urgency to go beyond Sunday sermons and prayers that seemed so limiting. And yet to "go into the world" was frightening; if I did "go," what would I do?

In the fall of 1986 I was accepted into a forty-week pastoral counseling training program with the Canadian Association for Pastoral Education. It was an intense learning experience with persons of all faiths, both as students and supervisors. We studied psychology, theology, counseling models, did approximately a hundred hours of supervised counseling, and were required to undergo our own psychotherapy with a certified psychologist. This experience continues to be a powerful resource in my life, for my family, and for my ministry both inside and outside the church.

Since ordination I have also completed almost 200 hours of Temple School courses, attended workshops on neurolinguistics, stress, loss, grief therapy, human sexuality, and marriage preparation counseling. I still doubt that I know enough but realize that it is now time to start "doing."

Of course, I continue to serve within the church in a variety of ways. There are some new dimensions of counseling as well as teaching and worship. I have been affirmed and supported both by the membership and the priesthood since my ordination. On occasion I have sensed that although some of my male colleagues intellectually approve of women's ordination, they do at times struggle on an emotional level and are not altogether sure where and how to "fit me in."

I still have more questions than answers—I always will! I relate to Moses' burning bush experience: "Who shall I say sends me?" and "Who am I to be sent?" My lot seems to be to "study it out." Such reflection always leads to an affirmation that I am called, in spite of my doubts, to function in Christ's image by enabling others to "have life and have it more abundantly."

Lori Combs
Independence, Missouri

My father was a Center Stake delegate at the 1984 World Conference, and he came home to tell us of the mood of his fellow delegates. My mother and I were astonished to hear that God would be calling women to the priesthood.

Personally, I did not like the idea. I was not strongly opposed, just uncomfortable. The more my father shared how the Holy Spirit rested on the Conference in relation to this issue, the more I accepted the idea of women priesthood members. After all, "All are called according to the gifts of God unto them" (D. and C. 119:8b). I was fifteen at the time of that Conference. Little did I know I would be a part of this historic movement.

I was deeply involved in Zion's League and loved the association with other church youth. I enjoyed doing things for other people and felt that God was pleased. The possibility of priesthood service never entered my mind until a trip I took with a group of Zion's Leaguers in the summer of 1986.

We toured the church's major historical sites in Kirtland, Palmyra, and Nauvoo. A turning point for me came in Kirtland. I had wanted God to do something magnificent and showy at our special service in the Temple. My mood was expectant; I wanted the same kind of experience felt by so many others in that structure ever since its dedication.

The service was wonderful, but I didn't realize it then. I had blinded myself and did not recognize the wonderful Spirit that abided with us. Our leader even told us that there were priesthood calls for our group, but I still did not think of myself. At the end of the service I felt God had betrayed me, leaving me utterly alone. Afterward, we all went outside to the beautiful garden next to the Temple. My friends knew that I was upset and sought to console me. I seriously thought about turning my back on all this "church stuff." Then, as we all looked up to the cloudy, night sky, a rainbow appeared. I was reminded of God's promise of hope and felt reassured that God had not given up on me.

Later, in Nauvoo, our youth leader asked me what I had expected at the Kirtland service. I confessed that I wanted some type of "lightning bolt" experience. He advised me to remember that worship service because it would become important in the near future. I did not understand, but I accepted his advice.

When I returned home I seriously thought about the possibility of priesthood service. Even then I saw it only as a remote, future event. By the time it came, *if* it did, I would be considerably more knowledgeable about God and the scriptures. I began to question my father about the processing of a priesthood call. He readily supplied all the information I needed. I confided in him that I felt as if I were standing on the edge of something. Little did I know that soon I would find myself going through a new doorway.

It was mid-August 1986 when I attended Wednesday prayer service as usual with my family. As I sat in the service, I was assailed with doubts. My soul seemed to be under attack from all the questions and doubts I had about God and my life's purpose. When the final hymn was sung, I emerged from my contemplation.

After the service my father, who was then pastor of

our congregation, called my mother and me into his office. He told us of my call to the office of deacon. The enormity of the situation truly weighed on my shoulders. My mother told me that my call helped her to accept the idea of women in the priesthood. She said that earlier it was as if God had told her, "After all, your daughter will be called." I was touched by their testimonies, but I had to know for myself.

I prayed and meditated for two days. I received a quiet assurance that this was of God. I informed my dad of my decision to accept the call and asked him to be the spokesman at my ordination.

I visited the stake youth director to tell him about the call. He already knew about it. I told him I did not quite understand why I was called to be a deacon since I did not see myself as a janitor, which is what I thought a deacon was. During our conversation I began to understand that a deacon sees to the physical well-being of the congregation. Something in me responded to *that* call.

The first female of the Center Stake youth to be called to a priesthood office, I was seventeen years old and nervous at the stake conference. So many people had gathered that it had to be held in the Auditorium conference chamber. One family friend told me she thought all the negative votes in the stake had showed up. My nervousness increased.

When the priesthood calls came up for consideration, mine was the first on the list. The presider asked for a show of cards in favor of the call. (Because there was some fear that people from outside the stake might come to vote against priesthood calls, cards were issued before the meeting only to those whose names appeared on the membership list.) He called for opposing votes, and then he announced the vote had passed. Someone asked for a recount by separate reporting of each section of the conference. I sat in an uncomfortable silence as the votes were counted once again and began to think of what would happen if my call was not approved. They were not pleasant thoughts. Thank God the vote passed again! Nevertheless, a separate count was taken on each of the women's calls but on none of the men's. All the calls passed.

Since my ordination in December 1986, my mother, too, has been called to the priesthood with the responsibilities of an elder. This entire experience has changed my life. Now I approach situations as a minister and try to visualize what a minister should do in each situation. I am no longer responsible just for myself but also for the physical and spiritual well-being of the people around me. The fact that I will be held accountable for this can weigh heavily on my shoulders, but the joy of serving my Lord always overcomes this feeling.

So far, no one has responded negatively to the ministry I have to offer. I feel confident that acceptance of women priesthood members will come because it is what the Lord wants. I am willing to wait on Christ and let him direct my paths. He has changed my life.

Linda L. (Troyer) Comstock
North Bend, Oregon

I will never forget that phone call from my father, Evangelist Luther Troyer, during the 1984 World Conference. He said a document had been presented to the delegates. The Temple could become a reality in my lifetime, and the priesthood were admonished to become dedicated to God's purposes. Then, in a quiet, sad voice, he told me the way was now open for women to be ordained.

My first thought as tears came was, Am I going to have to leave this church I have been raised in, believed in so deeply, and cherished so much? Dad said only that we must support our prophet, Wallace B. Smith, yet I could read the same anguish in his voice. But when I actually read Section 156 later, there was such a beautiful spirit in all the words. Something deep inside me told me I had to explore and understand them.

When I was a young girl I chose to serve my Lord by becoming a nurse. This would be a way to become a missionary in some exotic place in South America. I even took Spanish for several years plus college preparatory courses. A woman did not have to be ordained to care for the hungry, sick, and dying in another country, so it never mattered that women were not in the priesthood. My life did not lead to those exotic paths. I now realize I can serve wherever I am.

I shortly discovered hospital nursing did not fulfill my desires, so I began work with the elderly. They have so much to teach us and are so worthy of our respect and love. I have worked in nursing homes, home health departments, a hospice, and now with the State of Oregon Senior Service Division. I am grateful God has given me a gift of love for people in all walks of life. I can freely hug and love someone ragged, smelly, wrinkled, poverty stricken, and with a different skin color as easily as I can hug and love a beautiful, healthy, clean, young person.

It was not an easy year in 1984 as I sought to come to grips with the issue of ordaining women. I did not mention my concerns to anyone, even my husband, who was the pastor. I did not want my opinions to reflect or influence his own searching. I knew my father was experiencing turmoil, so I did not share with him or my mother. As I agonized I studied the scriptures and many books intently and listened as others shared their views. I still yearned to serve God, but I did not understand what that would mean in my life.

My father, who had been an appointee all my life, became ill, and I traveled to Kansas City to be with him. He was in an intensive care unit five weeks until his death in January 1986.

As a nurse I had never seen anyone suffer as much as he did. The stress of living in Independence with the turmoil of Section 156 had become a great burden to him. Having dear friends on both sides of the issue tore him apart and probably contributed to his high blood pressure and, ultimately, to his death. My mother understood this struggle, so she tried to bring peace at his funeral by choosing three pallbearers from each side of the issue to stand side by side. Reconciliation would still be his primary desire.

The first Saturday back in Oregon after the funeral, my husband told me I had been approved for a calling to the office of teacher. I could not stop the tears.

I am seldom emotional, but at that moment I felt utterly drained, overwhelmed, and unworthy. I wondered how the Lord could possibly use me as I felt I had nothing left to give anyone. I told my husband I would need a few days to answer. One morning as I drove to work pondering this, I realized my whole desire through the years had been to serve. I would need to trust God for strength and wisdom.

The office of teacher fascinated me as a child. I often wondered why there were not more of them in the church to handle internal conflicts. I had always wanted to be a peacemaker who calmed and uplifted others. Because God has given me the gift of empathy, it seemed right to accept that calling.

My professional training in college and as a nurse provided courses in grief, dying, alcohol and drug addiction, and crisis counseling. These, plus the three required Temple School courses, helped me prepare. The time since my ordination has been the most challenging of my life. I do not have more answers but only more questions. I want to be more disciplined in fasting, study, prayer, meditation, and searching as I realize the source of all my strength and power is God.

For the past three years, I have participated in providing training seminars out of the Oregon State Hospital geropsychiatric unit. This has improved my skills with the public, my own realm of knowledge, and my reputation as one supporting the worth and respect of seniors. My co-trainer is a female ordained minister in another denomination. Our friendship has allowed me to explore and share in many ways, including spiritual insights. God continues to open doors through mysterious ways. I do not yet know where this will someday lead.

My roughest times come when I am drained, weary, and down. I do not feel like socializing, visiting, or giving any more. I struggle then to cope with guilt. I know this is normal, but I do not like these feelings causing separation from God. Also, there can be times of great loneliness in this ministry. Especially in this small mission, I wish I had a company of committed members to carry out great ideas.

If there was one wish I would have as a new priesthood member, it would be for a mentor—some person to share with who could guide me. So few understand the calling and office of teacher. I struggle to know how and when to intervene in lives of people when I sense great need. At times I am afraid of causing more harm than good, so I hesitate.

New and exciting challenges continue to open before me. In late 1988 I accepted a call to the office of elder and was elected pastor for my branch. I am humbled to be part of God's work in some small way where I live and work.

Joann Condit
Phoenix, Arizona

Never once, in the many areas where I served throughout the church since 1952, have I felt neglected or discriminated against because I did not hold priesthood office. Quite frankly, it never occurred to me. I always felt that I held the success or failure of my husband's priesthood in my hands and that it was a real and vital responsibility. He had been ordained a priest, elder, seventy, and, finally, a president of Seventy. Our children were taught to honor and respect that priesthood and *always* support their father in his work for the Lord.

In the late 1970s a young man began attending services at our congregation. Several others and I helped him through some rough times. When this man made his decision for baptism, he was asked who he wished to baptize him. His response was, "I want Jo." Of course, he was told that Jo could not baptize him. He said, "I know that, but you asked me who I wanted...." Everyone laughed and the planning for the service went on. I could not laugh.

With his request I felt as though I had been filled with light, and I *felt*—not heard—the directive that indeed I *should* be the person to baptize and confirm him. This said to me that I had a calling to the office of elder. Yet how flatly this describes what was to me a soul-shaking experience.

That was about five years before Section 156 was given, and it was most disturbing to me. I struggled so hard with my feelings of "thinking more highly of oneself than one ought to think" and, indeed, the whole concept of women being called to priesthood responsibility. I did not even want to consider it and told no one of the experience. Even though I did my best to bury it, that thought came to my mind frequently and persistently.

My feeling on hearing the part of the revelation concerning ordination of women might best be described as dismay—even dread—for I *knew* that responsibility was upon me, and it seemed too heavy even to contemplate. Gradually over the next two years I came to realize that what God willed, he would also give strength to accomplish.

My call to the office of elder would have been processed early in 1985, but our assignment as a World Church appointee couple was changed to the Phoenix area. It was decided not to act on that call because we would be moving. No indication of this call was forwarded to the Arizona jurisdiction nor was I informed. But in May 1986, I was informed of the call to priesthood responsibility which came through the associate pastor of the Thunderbird Congregation of the Phoenix Metropole.

The ordination service itself was a tremendously uplifting experience, especially for me, my husband Clayton, and all our children who were able to come from other states. The congregation spilled over into the aisles and the lobby.

One part of that beautiful service which stands out most clearly in my mind occurred when the regional administrator included the following in his charge to the ordinands: "Remember, you have been called by God. And you have been called *by name.*" I shall never forget the certainty that flooded me at that time. And I have never regretted the acceptance of the responsibility that was placed on me.

My husband and I have found great joy in serving

together in new and unique ways, and we have found particular joy in the ordinance of administration to the sick. We have had several remarkable experiences in this area, but perhaps one particularly stands out.

We had gone to the hospital to visit a member, Mel, who had had surgery for colon cancer some months previously. This hospital stay was to reverse his colostomy. We had chatted for a short time when Mel asked Clay to administer to him. There was a pause of a few seconds, and then Mel said with an air of surprise, "Oh! Jo can be a part of this, too!" And he added that he wasn't accustomed to having a woman available for this ordinance just yet.

Mel told me later, "Jo, when you laid your hands on my head, I saw a shaft of light (measuring, with his finger and thumb joined, a circle about four to five inches across)—not solid light but like hundreds of tiny arrows of light. That light entered through the top of my head and spread all through my body. I saw it go around all the organs in my body, and then I heard the Lord say, 'If you live, you live unto me: if you die, you die unto me.'" Mel's face was alight with the joy of that experience, and he asked me if he might share that with other people, particularly those few in our area struggling with Section 156. I assured him that it was his testimony, and he, indeed, should share it. I added that I was afraid people would not believe him. He said that people knew he had no imagination and they would just *have to* believe him! He certainly has been valiant in his testimony.

I have gone from a passive sort of ministry—doing what I was told to do—to a much more aggressive ministry which reaches out and accepts all sorts of new responsibility. I have often been nervous and sometimes frightened of these new areas of service. I was quite hesitant to serve the Communion emblems, for example. I am not sure why, but I was most unsure of myself. It is so different to be on "the other side of the trays," and I needed both the assurance from God and the reassurance given me by other priesthood members.

A truly joyous experience came with the blessing of our newest grandson in April 1988. Clay assisted in the ordinance, and he held the baby up on his shoulder. I remember a grandmotherly smoothing of the cloth under Tyler's little chin before the blessing and leaning down to kiss his cheek after the blessing. In between I remember only what I must call "L-shaped light." I had such a sensation of light descending on me, through my head and shoulders, and making an L-shaped bend through my arms and hands to Tyler. I never knew a blessing could be such an experience and had never perceived that to be so before in all the blessings I've witnessed. Priesthood is a learning experience!

I am not sure what the Lord will require of me. I definitely feel my call to preaching and teaching ministry, to hospital and grief ministry, to a general loving and caring for people. Perhaps those things, outside of the sacraments of the church, will not be terribly different from those things I have done for years. Of one thing I am certain, however: my ministry will be deeper, fuller, and richer, enhanced by God's Spirit and power. I have already experienced that. Ministry on *this* side of ordination *is* different.

Elaine Constance
Stanley, Kansas

I have felt loved since I was a small child and took for granted that everyone loved me. I have a great love for people and have always felt confident that I could do anything I was asked to do. I don't know what my parents ever said or did to give me that sense of self-worth, but I am forever grateful and wish I had the formula to share it with the world. Even though I am a confident person, I know I have limitations and weaknesses. I rely on my Creator.

The last ten years have brought trials in my life that caused me to rely even more on God because of the helplessness I felt in these situations. I have become more compassionate and understanding of others' problems and needs as a result of these experiences. Many of these trials were related to the suffering of our children. It is painful for parents to see their children suffer and to be helpless in the situation.

In the past I always felt negative in conversations about women in the priesthood. I have always been proud of our priesthood. On Communion Sundays, as the men made their way down the aisle and took their place in the service, my heart filled with love and admiration. The thought of women going down the aisle with that group was not in my thinking.

With the introduction of Section 156, my feelings and thoughts were challenged. Although I was totally content with a male priesthood, I remembered how I had been ministered to time and time again by women through teaching, talks, classes, music, and their daily loving acts toward me. I struggled with women being in the priesthood. But because of my faith, my belief in the prophet, and our system within the church, I knew that I had to search my soul and change my thinking. God is so far ahead of us. How could I think I knew more than God? So I started my journey of acceptance.

When I was told of my call, I felt many emotions—fear, inadequacy, joy—and cried. I prayed and read from the Doctrine and Covenants, looking for every scripture that used the word "elder." I wanted to understand better what would be required of me and was overcome with my inadequacies. As I prayed, a happiness flowed through my body, and the Spirit filled me. I then knew that God had called me.

When my priesthood call came and before I accepted, I spoke with a Catholic friend, Joann, and asked her to remember me in her prayers. We have been best friends for twenty-five years. She invited me over for a social evening, and when I arrived, there were three other RLDS friends, one of my daughters, and eight Catholic friends. This was a surprise prayer service for me in support of my priesthood. She had planned a service with an Advent centerpiece on the table. Music was played which had been written and sung by Catholic monks. As we stood around the table, each person either prayed for me or gave an encouraging testimony regarding my priesthood. Joann had gotten hymnals from our church, and we sang "The Old Old Path." She read John 15:16, "Ye have not chosen me, but I have chosen you, and ordained you, that ye should go and bring forth fruit...", then closed with a prayer. What a beautiful memory to have this dear Catholic friend do this for me at a special time in my life!

I am traveling on a journey of trust. I have presided, administered to the sick, confirmed new members, and preached. What I feared most was administering to the sick. My prayer beforehand would always be that my faults and inadequacies would not stand in the way of God's blessing and that as God's instrument, a blessing would flow.

As I assisted in administering to a three-year-old boy, a combination of humility and joy attended me. Following the administration, the little boy smiled and we hugged. His grandmother came to me fifteen minutes later saying she had asked the boy if he needed a cold cloth on his head and a drink of water. His reply was, "I don't need it now, Grandma; Jesus made me well." Experiences like these fill me with even more humility, and I thank God for allowing me to be a part of this beautiful ordinance.

A young woman attended our church for the first time on the day of my ordination. Later, when she was baptized, she asked me to confirm her. As I laid my hands upon her head, the Spirit of God filled me to such an extent that I trembled throughout my whole body. Because my husband was assisting, I moved my fingers to touch him for support during the prayer. The words flowed, my mind was clear, and a great blessing came to me. By the way, that young woman has since become my daughter-in-law.

I have observed priesthood women in action. My heart swells with joy as I see the ministry they bring. I have heard it said that we do not serve as male elders do; we serve as women who are elders with a somewhat different ministry.

I feel I have been given the gift of love, and I see this as my main ministry. I want to continue to be aware of others' needs and to carry their concerns on my heart as if they were my own. I anticipate the gifts which will be given to me as I move out to serve as an elder and as I am called upon to give ministry in ways I have not yet had opportunity to give. God is my partner in my journey of faith and trust, and I am grateful to respond according to that divine purpose and grace.

Lois Marie Davis
Ocean Springs, Mississippi

I know that God continually has led me in directions of service. Having always been a part of this church, I have at times taken for granted the workings of the Holy Spirit in my life. God has always been there, and I have expected that guidance in my life.

I can remember as a young child sitting in services and listening to the music being played on the piano; my greatest desire was to play piano and make beautiful music. I took music lessons, and by the age of thirteen I could play in the congregation. I was music director for years, and also have taught Sunday school classes from primary age through adult. I have found that the best way to learn is to serve. Each thing I do gives me the desire to do more. I have always loved working in the church because it was the one place I was secure. Through this work I was strengthened to withstand the pressures of the world itself.

When the Faith to Grow program was begun, I became the worship commission chairperson and moved into a leadership role for the worship services. Again, I was being molded and prepared.

In April 1986 my district president and pastor came to my home to talk with me. I knew what it was about, and I was *scared*. I had always said that I didn't think women should be ordained because the burden was too heavy, and we were already carrying a full load. It wasn't fair that women should have to do it all. I especially resented people "pushing" women's ordination.

When the direction came at the 1984 World Conference, I was dumbfounded at first. I was a delegate that year and certainly not expecting it. I remember looking at the person sitting next to me and asking, "What did he say? Did I hear him right?" When I got back to my motel room I immediately called home. I told my mother and asked her to pray about it because we would be voting later in the week, and I just did not know what to do. Then I prayed, and I prayed, and when the time came to vote such a sense of peace and reassurance filled me that I knew the Spirit was confirming to me the truth of this revelation. I felt a stirring of joy and excitement that is hard to describe. At the instant I raised my hand in support, a still, small voice spoke to me—I had a calling to the office of elder. Then I felt fear, for I did not feel worthy or capable. I remember thinking, "No, no, I don't want it. It's too much. I do enough. I don't want to do any more. I don't want it."

After that Conference I made sure that everyone, especially my branch president, knew that I did not want to be called. I was Jonah running away. In my mind I had decided that if everyone knew how I felt, I wouldn't be called. Of course, it didn't work, because God knew my heart and knew I wouldn't say no. I knew the reason for my calling, and I knew I could not deny the people of Ocean Springs the additional ministry I could give them through my receiving the Melchisedec priesthood. Perhaps I was just trying to postpone the event, and, of course, it didn't last for long.

God, in love and mercy, had given me the "breathing space" I needed to come to terms with my call to elder. Ocean Springs had been praying a long time for more priesthood. I looked at my congregation—at all those people I love so much and who love me—and I knew I had a greater service to them. I had been serving them in different ways since I was thirteen. Now I could serve them in an additional way and fill a greater need.

Following my ordination service we had potluck dinner, which gave us the opportunity to visit with everyone there. Some of my friends from other denominations had come to share this experience. I was so happy that they wanted to share this with me. I felt I was "off the ground" all day. It was wonderful and exhausting.

I served as counselor to the branch president in Ocean Springs in 1987 and was elected pastor for 1988. I was scared, for it was totally new ground and a heavy burden. But I know that God's Spirit is with me, guiding me. Sometimes God has been with me so strongly that it has overwhelmed me. The blessings of the Holy Spirit have truly been mine as I have attempted to do God's work. The more I do, the more I am blessed. I am thankful God is able to use me.

Edith Joy (Parker) Dawson
McAllen, Texas

When I was about six, two missionaries visited our home. They brought stories, films, and many beautiful shells with them from the South Sea islands. I remember wondering why women weren't allowed such joyous travels and experiences. Even as a child, I was concerned about the inequality of women's roles in the church and in life.

Because of home problems, my family attended church sporadically, but my mother's faith during my childhood provided me with a sure basis that God was at work in the church. As for my own children, I witnessed all four sons baptized; three eventually held priesthood.

I worked in the church during my adult life, but there seemed to be little joy. My life was filled with tragedy, problems, failures, and burdens, mostly brought on by myself. Yet through all of this, I continued to experience God working in my life.

I moved from Missouri to the Rio Grande Valley in southern Texas to teach Mexican-American migrant students to read. In 1982 I again became concerned that women were not assuming church leadership roles they were capable of filling. I didn't really know what I wanted for women, but I saw generally that they were not allowed to grow to their full potential. They were often relegated to the nursery and kitchen, raising money at bake sales, and cleaning floors and toilets. Though I did not think these things were unimportant, I wondered why men were always the speakers, directors, administrators, keepers of the money, and the travelers.

This type of thinking wasn't acceptable in my home branch, so I decided to drive the thirty-five miles from my home to Weslaco, Texas. Immediately, I was asked to serve on the worship commission planning services, and I also was given an adult class to teach.

During the summer of 1986 I went to the Lake of the Ozarks in Missouri to work on a house that I was building for my retirement. The house was only framed in and had no electricity or water. It was pitch dark in the house that first night, but I put an air mattress by an open door and slept peacefully. I listened to the night sounds and found relief from a difficult school year. I was awakened during the night by these words being burned into my brain: "I have more important things for you to do than building this house."

I began to sense a call to the priesthood even though I couldn't understand it. My life just didn't merit such for me. There had been too many mistakes. No one who knew of my past could accept me—surely!

Upon returning to the Rio Grande Valley for the 1986-87 school year, my pastor came by my home to tell me I had been called to the office of priest. He listened to all my protests then gently told me to pray about it.

And pray I did! I slept fitfully for nights, asking God over and over if this was a true call. Would I be more of a hindrance than a help? Would my freedom be taken away from me? I wondered as I thought of the responsibility that would be mine. At the same time, I was being washed with a sense of joy and remembrance of the experiences in my past that pointed to this call. Acceptance came, although there were no other dreams or words. I knew I was to respond to this call of God in my life.

The ordination service in October 1987 was a bittersweet one. I had spent the previous night listening to my sons express deep concerns about the church, and I had prayed most of the night for my children. On the other hand I was so thankful they had come to support me on this special day. A portion of the ordination prayer was offered in Spanish, which meant something to me because I've always loved the Spanish-speaking people, and I speak some Spanish myself. My two sons offered beautiful prayers on my behalf. During the service I found myself praising and feeling close to God, while at the same time I yearned for my children to respond more fully to God and the church.

There's something different about my life now. Doing things in front of people has never been of great enjoyment to me. And yet, as I have prepared for Wednesday evening responsibilities, invocations, offerings, and sermons, the Lord has rested upon me as though I'm shielded by an aura from all of that fear, and I find that I can speak of godly things without excessive trembling. I have felt blessed with insight while listening to people talk about their problems. I see each person's worth more than I used to and find myself saying things that need to be said and are of some help. There is a gift of the Spirit that is with me that helps me bring a different ministry than before.

Priesthood service has been the greatest experience of my life. I dreaded turning sixty, but, instead, life is really just beginning. Oh, I still get angry. I'm still selfish at times, but I'm growing and learning with a new joy that stems from personal knowledge of what great things God can do in the lives of people, regardless of environmental background or weaknesses and failures. God has done great things in my life, too. Thank you, God, for allowing me to be a part of building Zion for a world in need.

Melba Jean Dixon
Farwell, Michigan

During the weeks which followed the 1984 World Conference, I began to have positive feelings concerning women's ordination. I looked forward with anticipation to the calling of many young women who seemed ready and eager to accept priesthood responsibility. I felt safe in assuming that women my age would not be called.

This pleased me as I have always felt an uneasiness with public ministry. In the past my greatest joy has been to pray and to plan a worship service, to enlist personnel to carry out the various duties, then to sit back in the congregation and share in the Spirit which moved among the people, enabling them to experience a closer relationship with God.

Shortly after I returned home from Conference, I began to develop an overwhelming desire to study the scriptures. Thoughts of being called to the priesthood began entering my mind—thoughts which I attempted to dismiss because the idea frightened me. One day as I knelt in prayer, the image of myself functioning in the priesthood passed before me, similar to an experience I had before my father's death. From that time on, I somehow knew that I would be called.

On the morning my pastor walked into our home to tell me I had been called, I knew why he was there. He shared with me that he felt I had a calling as an elder but that I should be ordained first to the office of priest. My response was that I would give the matter serious consideration. On the same day he informed my mother that she had a calling as a teacher.

I spent several weeks in prayer and fasting. During this time I traveled to the Michigan Region Office with my district president. He shared that he had received evidence of our callings long before our names were submitted. He told me that if I was not ordained an elder at that time, I would be called to that office in the near future. This agreed with my experience in which I saw myself administering the laying on of hands. My mother and I soon accepted our calls. My husband, who is a deacon, and my three sons gave their support.

On the morning our calls were presented to the membership, several persons stood in support of our callings. One woman, who previously had been opposed to women's ordination, testified that she had read Section 156 that morning and had received evidence of its truthfulness. Our calls were approved, and we were ordained at the Farwell Church in November 1986. My three brothers, all elders, officiated at the service.

I have had many positive experiences since then. My ministry was accepted readily, and I have found there is a tremendous need for ministry to families and children in our area. I feel God's presence with me as I carry out the duties of my office and calling.

Many opportunities for ministry have come my way, including officiating at two weddings. In both instances I felt the couples requested that I officiate as a result of the inherent qualities of acceptance and empathy I possess as a woman. Because the Holy Spirit blessed us all so richly on both occasions, I am convinced more than ever that my priesthood calling is to minister in love to the bruised and brokenhearted.

Truly, the Holy Spirit moves in wondrous ways in

our lives. I place no limits upon our future possibilities. My only desire is that I may grow to be a more capable servant of the Lord I love, ministering to his people wherever they stand in need.

Florence (Toovey) Dreher
Weyburn, Saskatchewan, Canada

I was serving as district women's consultant and had organized a women's retreat in the Weyburn Church that weekend. It had been well received, and we were having a rewarding experience. The district president and his wife were our guest ministry, and they were staying in our home. So when he and my husband, Vernon, who is our pastor, asked to talk with me, I just assumed it was to complete plans for the Sunday morning worship service.

When they informed me of my priesthood call, I think if I had not been sitting down I would have fallen. I had thought when the first group of women were ordained that would be it for the time being. Perhaps I was even a bit relieved that I had not been called, as I did not feel worthy.

I was skeptical and had many doubts when I first heard Section 156 had passed. Yet I believed in the prophet and that this is Christ's church, so I undertook much searching and praying for assurance. I had been quite active in a leadership capacity in my branch and district for a number of years in youth and women's work, blessed with an outpouring of the Spirit on many occasions, for which I have felt very humble and thankful. I know that the success of all our efforts was because God's Spirit graced us and those with whom we were working in our various endeavors.

During my struggles with the new revelation, I had a dream that made me realize how wrong I had been in my doubting. I dreamt I was in a large room with several others who were having difficulty with Section 156. As we reasoned and shared together, it seemed from time to time someone, unseen by me, would come and usher some of the others out. I knew these people had become convinced of the revelation's truth. After several people were taken away, I cried out, "Why doesn't someone come and help me?" A voice clearly said, "Because you have the power within to help yourself." When I woke the next morning the whole world seemed beautiful and full of possibilities.

Even though I was overwhelmed by the call, I had no doubt but that it was of God, and I was eager to get into the work. During the service in August 1986 when I was ordained as an elder, the soloist sang the words, "And I know you'll walk with Jesus all the way." An indescribable feeling came over me, and I truly wanted to let Christ be my guide. I shall not forget this experience of musical worship nor the service itself.

My family members were all supportive of my call. As we visited and shared with them, they responded with, "You can do it Mom." They seemed more sure of my capabilities than I. But knowing that God had seen me through many times of stress and trials, I knew I could depend on that same source of strength in the future.

I am keenly aware that we are to be an example for others in our daily walk of life. It scares me a little to know that our lives are being observed daily. I only hope and pray that I will never let anything creep into my life that will cause anyone to doubt me.

I am active in two nondenominational groups—one a Bible-study group that meets every Wednesday morning. Our sharing has been meaningful, and many times I have been asked to explain my understanding of certain scriptures. I am so thankful that on these occasions God has supplied me with insight that has filled the need. Being on the executive committee of the other group has given me the opportunity to have our women provide an afternoon of devotion and sharing with these ladies. It constantly brings joy to me because I know that this has been brought about by the movement of Christ's loving Spirit.

As elders, Vernon and I have had the joy of serving people together in our home branch as well as in the district and region. This is a constant joy. As a young person I always wanted to be a missionary. When Vernon was called to the priesthood, I was thrilled. I thought that together we could work for our Lord, and we did for a number of years. But now it is a greater joy as we work together in this new way. I am excited and really looking forward to the future when we can be of greater service to God's people.

I find it different being in the priesthood. On many previous occasions I have given talks in our home branch and elsewhere. But now, as I prepare to share on a Sunday morning, there seems to be a greater responsibility. I'm not sure why this is because I know God has directed me in messages I have given before. Maybe I feel that people are expecting more. Whatever it is, I know if I remember that God is in charge, it will work out all right.

Emily Dunsdon
Tabor, Iowa

Counsel in my patriarchal blessing, given when I was twenty-two, has been a special guide throughout my adult life: "Take advantage of every opportunity also to serve your heavenly Father." Throughout my life I have attempted to do this to the best of my ability and have been steady in my commitment over the forty years we've lived in Tabor, Iowa.

One of the first questions my husband-to-be asked me was, "What church do you belong to, and how important is it to you?" He proposed to me on our third date! We have been married for forty years. A good, supportive spouse is necessary for a priesthood calling. I supported him in his ministry as deacon, and he has been supportive of mine as an elder.

We live on a farm, and it was necessary for me to work outside the home to "make ends meet." I planned my vacations in order to take our two sons to reunions, conferences, and youth camps while my husband stayed home to care for the livestock. We enjoyed serving together as Zion's League leaders for several years while our boys were growing up.

When Section 156 was presented to the 1984 World Conference, I felt the Holy Spirit flood my soul. I knew this revelation was God's will, and the feeling was confirmed to me that I would be one of the women called to the priesthood. I immediately began to study to be prepared for my calling when it came. But the call didn't come and didn't come, yet I was sure I had a call to the office of elder. My husband also had confirmation of this call and couldn't understand why it was taking so long. Other women in our congregation were called, and I later learned that our pastor had difficulty with priesthood calls for a female to a so-called "higher office" than that held by her husband.

I should add, however, that under this pastor I have had various opportunities for growth and ministry. I served as leadership commissioner, priesthood training officer, historian, secretary, women's leader, adult church school teacher, church school director, and as a member of the RLDS Social Services Advisory Board in the stake.

Following the appointment of a new pastor, my call was completed and approved at an Omaha-Council Bluffs Stake conference. Six weeks later I was ordained in Tabor, Iowa, by my two sons. A sister-in-law who was opposed to women's ordination attended. I was surprised she was there and commented to her, "I thought you didn't believe." She answered, "I don't, but I believe in you." What a blessing!

The Holy Spirit continues to confirm to me that it is God's will for women to be members of the priesthood. I thank God for a prophet strong enough to present God's will to the people, even if divisiveness results.

I seem to struggle much harder than before my ordination to find time to study, concentrate, and be "about my Father's business." It bothers me when my thoughts wander as I try to pray and when I procrastinate and do less than my best at an assignment because I don't budget my time.

One member of my congregation told me I was an unfriendly person because I didn't greet or visit with the members after the worship service and seemed aloof and uncaring. Perhaps it was because I am usually emotionally drained after teaching a class or giving a sermon. Now I make an effort to say something personal to each one and be more friendly.

I find that I now seem to be the "clearing house" for church information. People tell me when and why they are going to be absent, who is ill and needs prayers, who is upset with another and needs counseling, and they ask my opinion on class materials, where to find a scripture, etc. I seldom used the telephone for anything but business before—a habit from twenty years of employment as an administrator. Now I try to "friendly visit" with someone every day.

I feel that women have unique talents and abilities that are not being used. Instead, women serve where men assign them in typical priesthood roles—presiding, assisting, preaching, and serving Communion. Although I have studied and prayed about this, I don't know what we should be doing differently, so I cannot complain. Perhaps time and temple ministries will help clarify this for us.

I do see women as nurturers, often blessed with a spirit of discernment. I believe all women members (priesthood or not) have an important role to play, especially in health, education, family planning, counseling, and teaching. In the past I saw the role of women only as pastoral caretakers—teaching children, leading choirs, and responsible for worship, basket dinners, and other such roles in the home congregation. I now feel women need to move into areas of outreach in communities, families, politics, environmental issues, economics, education, and any other field where people are in bondage and ignorance.

God has blessed and watched over me all the days of my life and continues to bless me in my endeavors of service. I am so thankful to be living in these latter days and look forward with anticipation to the future. I want to remain faithful and expand and enlarge my calling.

Carol L. Ergo
Saginaw, Michigan

There was a strong mixture of joy, awe, and some fear present in the atmosphere that Sunday morning in November 1985 when two other women and I were ordained as elders at the Center Road Church in Saginaw. The joy was in the commitment of our lives in answer to God's call, the awe of being a part of a history-making event, and the fear in the realization of the seriousness of this action and the effect it would have on the church body because of the antagonism of some members concerning women's ordination.

I first learned of my call in late August 1985. I accepted this responsibility the same day the pastor spoke to me about it. It did not come as a surprise because for many months the Holy Spirit had prepared me. About a year prior to this call, thoughts would come into my mind that this would happen in my life, and, at first, I attempted to reject this idea. I remember asking God, "Do you really want me to do this?" I could not deny that the revelation was God's direction to me and that this call would surely occur. Without this confirmation, I would not have had the courage or strength to be one of the first women ordained.

Although most members of our congregation and district supported the priesthood calls of women, there had been some opposition in the business meetings of both jurisdictions a short time before. Some people who voted negatively said they were voting against Section 156 and not against specific women. This was difficult for me to accept because some of the negative votes came from close friends of many years. When my husband and I shared my call to elder at a small gathering of our closest friends in the church, we were puzzled and upset by their reaction—shocked silence. There was not the usual presence of congratulatory, joyful exclamations we had observed when men were called to the priesthood. The reaction of the congregation was similar when the announcement was made from the pulpit the following Sunday.

When it became known that I was going to be ordained, one sister in the church asked me, "Carol, are you going to be a real elder?" A brother called me aside and expressed his concern over women's ordination, saying there surely would be problems in sexual matters if men and women worked together in the priesthood. Another sister wondered who would do the cooking and child rearing if women became too busy with church activities. Another commented that she would not want to be ordained because it would result in lessening the importance of ordained men.

During the past twenty-seven years I have held many offices in the church at congregational, district, and regional levels. I have always been an advocate of women's rights and have counseled women to assist them in working through their problems. I taught the Temple School course, "Women's Roles in Church and Society," where many questions were raised concerning women's place in the decision-making processes of the church. Yet finding acceptable answers was a difficult task.

A few years ago I believed I had contributed as much as possible to our church organization and that there was no more for me to do under the male-dominated system of that time. I felt frustrated to see what could and should be done but without power or authority to accomplish the task. Before publication of *Hymns of the Saints* I found many of our hymns difficult to sing because their expressions did not correspond with our professed theology of the worth of persons. I observed numerous injustices occurring around me, such as a man with ordinary abilities being called to the priesthood while his wife, who also was dedicated to the work of the church, committed to the gospel of Jesus Christ, and well-educated, was ignored.

I recall being amazed and somewhat shocked at my first World Conference in 1972, when, on Monday morning, most of the men rose from their chairs and left the conference chamber. I whispered to the delegate next to me, "Where are they going?" I could hardly believe that all of these men would be going to special quorum meetings to discuss and make decisions concerning the current issues before us, and the remaining elected and well-informed delegates (the nonordained ones and, therefore, mostly women) were not included. This bias in the church has been frustrating and disheartening.

Since my ordination my work has expanded into areas not available to me previously. This expansion has been a natural progression of my life's work. The response of the people to my ministry as an ordained or unordained person has been essentially the same. No one has been abusive or unkind or to my knowledge has refused to participate in church activities in which I have been involved.

One of my most outstanding experiences as a priesthood member was when I participated in serving Communion during the 1986 World Conference.

Because I had been ordained the previous November, my experience in serving Communion was minimal. I felt inadequate and almost declined the invitation to take part. However, I felt compelled to be part of this historic event. When the servers gathered early that morning outside the conference chamber, the same atmosphere of ordination day was present—one of joy, awe, and apprehension. These feelings were heightened by the counsel we were given concerning the disruptions that could possibly arise.

As I sat down in my row next to two male priesthood members, one of them remarked, "Well, I guess we have to move over and make way for the women." Because I had made a pact with myself not to acknowledge poor jokes and demeaning remarks, I did not react in any way to what he said. As the time drew near for the beginning of the service, I became more anxious when I realized that I would have to walk the entire length of the center aisle to take my place at the rear of the chamber. I wondered if I would be able to perform this ministry. I was afraid of making an error or being rejected by those people I would be serving. The realization that this task had to be performed not once but in each of the three scheduled services was almost more than I could cope with. The first service was somewhat tense, but after we experienced the joy of men and women serving together, side by side, everyone relaxed and could truly appreciate the uniqueness of what was occurring. The Holy Spirit was manifested powerfully that morning, and we were supported in love.

My current involvement in ministry has included administration to the sick and dying and counseling to the bereaved. This ministry has extended to my relationships with colleagues at school and in the community. Two of my most delightful "tasks" were the blessings of my grandchildren.

I am pleased to be given this new and expanded opportunity to serve God and the church; however, the task is great, and I often feel inadequate. My main desire and purpose in the work I do is to be a positive Christian influence in the lives of others in my church and community. The work is difficult, but the joy of service is an adequate reward.

Genevieve (Hougas) Francis
St. Joseph, Missouri

All my life I have had the supportive role for the priesthood members in my family: grandfather, father, brother, husband, son, son-in-law. I grew up in an appointee family (Ward Hougas was my father). My husband, Melvin, served as an appointee minister for twenty-nine years and is now an evangelist-patriarch. Serving the Lord has been a way of life and has brought much joy to my soul.

I still play a supportive role, but now I have the added responsibility of my own priesthood. This is indeed different; I know that God has asked me to do this, and I consider it an opportunity for continued service.

I honestly don't feel that what I am doing for the Lord today is any more important than the many things I have been doing in the past. It's just a different type of service! Surely teaching my children to walk uprightly before the Lord was of utmost importance, along with working with children and in youth camps. God calls each of us to do different things for him. At various times in our lives we have unique opportunities to work together for and with God. That is what is really important.

I have found much happiness in serving as an elder in the church. There are those who find it difficult to accept me as an elder—not many, but a few. Yet no one has ever been unkind to me. Besides working in my own congregation, I am assigned to preach in the stake about once a month. I had the joy of assisting in a beautiful church wedding. One morning I assisted a grandfather in the blessing of his grandson. My husband and I go as a team to administer to the sick; sometimes people come to our home for administration.

I appreciate the loving support of my husband. He has helped me in countless ways. I realize that with my ordination he had a great adjustment to make, but he has made it graciously. At times it has been difficult working with two priesthood schedules and just one car, but with patience and sacrifice my husband has made it possible for me to fulfill my assignments.

Giving ministry since my ordination has taken on new dimensions. But basically it is the same as before, trying to help people meet their physical and spiritual needs and, thereby, draw them closer to God. That is what ministry is all about. I believe the Lord has given me a special gift to recognize others' needs, and this is most helpful as I seek to give ministry. I find it a marvelous, challenging opportunity.

For years I heard people discuss the idea of women in the priesthood. I always thought I didn't need to be unduly concerned about this issue because *God does the calling*; if God wanted women in the priesthood, instructions would come through the prophet. Perhaps someday that might be an actuality, I thought. But on April 3, 1984, I discovered that "someday" had arrived. Two days later I knew I was helping to write history when I raised my hand in support of Section 156.

As the vote was taken that day, I felt God's beautiful Spirit of peace and love dwelling within me in a moving way. Many other delegates had the same experience. For lack of a better way of describing it, it was like rays of sunshine coming down from above to warm my body. Where there were clouds of doubt, the sunshine could not get through, so not everyone felt its warmth. That day I knew I had been touched by God's Spirit. I came home from the 1984 World Conference feeling uplifted, knowing without a doubt that God had indeed spoken to us through his prophet.

Almost two years went by, and I began hearing that some women were being called and ordained. At the 1986 Conference, as I was served the Communion emblems by a woman, I thought, This is good. I was thrilled to imagine additional responsibilities ordained women of the church could now help with. In many congregations the work load has rested heavily on only a few priesthood members, overworking them to their physical limits. Now the burden could be shared.

Like most women in the church, I wondered if I would be called to the priesthood. I even had people ask me that question, and I would laughingly say, "No, I'm too old, but I am certainly looking forward to younger women being called." Then I discovered that women even older than I were being called and ordained. I began to think soberly about the possibilities. As the next few weeks went by, I found myself thinking of being called to the office of elder. I couldn't get it out of my mind. I tried to suppress those feelings, thinking I was "seeking" priesthood, and I felt this was wrong. The more I tried to rid my mind of those thoughts, the stronger they became until I had nothing but turmoil within me.

One night as I lay in bed sleepless, the Holy Spirit filled my body again like sunshine coming from above. I was filled with the knowledge that God had been trying to tell me that indeed I was called to minister as an elder; that same spirit of peace that I had experienced at Conference was flooding my being again. The Lord knows I don't like surprises—I can handle things better if I am prepared for them—so God was preparing me.

During those weeks, God also was sending enlightenment to my pastor, who bears this testimony: he had made it a matter of prayer and study concerning women in the priesthood, and he received an answer one Sunday morning as he sat on the rostrum looking over the congregation. When his eyes fell on me, it came to him in such a way that there was no doubt in his mind that I had been called to the office of elder. He said that almost every time he saw me after that, the Spirit bore witness to him concerning my call.

I know that life will never be the same again, but I also know, through experiences I have had, that life is made up of changes. This is just one of many changes that requires some adjustment on my part; this time it presents me with a marvelous opportunity to serve my Lord.

Ruth Midgorden Goodwin
Fountain Valley, California

My presiding elder took me aside after a 9:30 a.m. worship service in October 1985 to tell me of my call as an elder. My husband had to be gone that afternoon, so I was home alone for a few hours. I felt such a tremendous spirit of peace, reassurance, confidence, and enablement. My mind centered on the kinds of things I would like to see happen in our church community and its geographic neighborhood—the needs of people.

This was not a wishing-for-the-moon experience devoid of realism, however, but included the limitations of my age and the abilities, training, and time restraints of others. The overall mindset I have come to identify with the Holy Spirit was expressing, "I will do the best I can and all I can for you, Lord." This may well be a universal experience for anyone who receives the Lord's invitation to follow.

I was ordained in January 1986 in the Costa Mesa Church by my brother and my husband. I felt wonderfully supported by the congregation as well as by friends, family, and neighbors who made the day special for me.

Part of the ordination prayer piqued my interest because the words, "when she presides," were interpreted by me at first as presiding over services. After all, I thought, I will never be a presiding elder; I am too old. How mistaken I was. In less than an year, I began a two-year term as presiding elder of my congregation—and this at the congregation's option! They chose me; I didn't choose the responsibility. Nevertheless, I am being granted the strength and the other necessary attributes for the task, and I have the strong support of men and women in our group.

I recall hearing rumors prior to the 1984 World Conference that something about women's ordination would come to the Conference floor. I was opposed because I presumed some jurisdiction was going to bring a resolution. But I was against it because of a more important aspect—the priesthood structure itself. Although I appreciated the commitment of many priesthood members, through the years I had grown increasingly disenchanted by the arrogance, incompetence, and indifference of many of the men holding priesthood office. I believed we would intensify and double the problem if we ordained women.

I remember a quick conversation sometime after my ordination with an apostle I know who asked, "Well, do you feel any different?" I responded, "Not really." We looked at each other and smiled. There are those who believe in some dramatic change when priesthood is conferred. I am not one of them. I have understood priesthood to be a concept of serving, of special enlightenment at times due to the office or the need of people, but God is working within the framework of each person's personality and gifts.

I have found greater freedom since being elected presiding elder. During the months of lining up leadership, working at goals and objectives, and the other tasks that go with this job, I felt my old confidence coming back to the fore. Although I have had periods of uncertainty and have never spoken publicly without apprehension and a certain amount of knee knocking, I can honestly say I felt that I could do what was required and do it reasonably well. I don't believe this is cockiness. I was taught early that intelligence and other such gifts are given by God and that much is required of those to whom much is given.

There is a sense in which I have had to learn—and still need to learn—to allow myself to function in my office. It is hard to overcome the strong indoctrination through the years which relegated males to one place and females to another. Supporting my husband in his calling as an evangelist-patriarch is important to me. And now he also is providing such valuable support for me. His commitment for the years I will be presiding elder is to help me in any way he can, just as I have helped him. He continues his own activities, of course, but our mutual commitment is to my pastoral responsibility, fitting other things around it.

I see my ministry as an enabling and facilitating one, to help the congregation grow spiritually and numerically, and to help people, especially priesthood, realize their own potential. Individuals have moved out to volunteer for certain tasks, and they have seemed to sense what those tasks are. We had an unusual goals-planning evening late in July during which a grass roots prophetic spirit seemed to move to bring the principle of common consent—subtly yet powerfully—to the fore in our midst. I am thankful for this cohesive spirit operating with most of us.

I have appreciated the support of my entire family, both immediate and cousin variety. I also want to express how fully the women in my congregation have backed me. If I perceive something under the surface correctly, I think they look at me as a trailblazer. Many of these women are in their seventies and eighties, but there is strong support for me even though there may be a couple who aren't quite sure women should be in the priesthood. I have never felt any indication of jealousy from them—only camaraderie. They and their companions are dependable, regular attenders who are willing to do whatever is within their power and strength to do. How I appreciate them!

I feel indebted to the World Church because of leaders and writers who so consistently have been changing my outlook on our mission as a church and on the concepts of ministry for the past twenty years or more. I have found that many persons in the church have stayed on one level from the time of baptism, dependent on one or more strong personalities who have told them what to believe and what not to believe. They have not understood that the church never did believe some of what they still espouse today as church doctrine.

We continue to change, sometimes almost imperceptibly, as we allow ourselves to be open to the influence of the Holy Spirit. My changes in thinking have been, for the most part, a quiet, almost intuitive process as I have listened, participated, and discussed issues. So many experiences throughout my life—before and since my ordination—have helped me grow in patience, compassion, and insight.

Charlotte D. Gould
Lamoni, Iowa

My call to the office of elder was presented to a Lamoni Stake conference in November 1986. My statement printed in the conference bulletin indicates my feelings regarding it:

"This priesthood call to me is much like the gesture of Jesus to his special servants as he called, 'Follow me.' It comes after almost a lifetime of experiences that have led me to this place, this moment, these circumstances. More than fifty years ago I was assured by the Spirit that there would always be work for me to do if I kept myself prepared and ready. In recent months I have had an intensification of the power of light and love and freedom as I have studied for special assignments. I want very much to be an acceptable steward. I accept this call with humility and even fear, but also with great joy. I pray that I may be worthy of the trust and responsibility."

I can see that many forces have worked together to prepare me for serving as an elder, although through the years there was no expectancy for that. After the death of my husband, Bill, in August 1969, I continued with some work he and I had begun after visiting the Orient in the summer of 1963 to study current methods of teaching English there.

Bill wrote a detailed report in which he recommended that the teaching of English be included in our evangelistic efforts in the Orient. As a result the English Language School, in conjunction with the church in Japan, was begun in Seijo, a section of Tokyo, in 1970. I helped in the planning of the curriculum that first year, and the following year I taught in the school and helped to establish some procedures and directions. For fourteen months I worked in the school and with the students' parents, assisted in the congregation, and lived with the Japanese people. Through reading and study of Japanese history, culture, religion, and life-style, I gained a deep understanding of what it could mean to really be a "world church."

Although I have grieved in my widowhood and spent many lonely hours, I have used some of those lonely times for such in-depth study of the scriptures as I had never experienced.

One life-changing experience for me was a visit in the late 1970s to Greece and Turkey with a group led by Velma Ruch. I was overwhelmed on touching the soil where the Apostle Paul had stood and faced tremendous obstacles establishing Christianity. I have always been somewhat romantic and imaginative, and I could stand beneath the ruins in the various cities and almost commune with Paul. I could see more clearly the problems he faced in moving Jews, Greeks, and Romans into the new ways of Christianity. As a result of that trip, I designed a winter's study based on the life and teachings of Paul which I used with a women's group of our congregation, the Goal Finders. Both the preparation and the teaching were exciting.

Twice during the 1970s I was asked to teach a Book of Mormon class in church school. I designed a course in which I tried to stimulate excitement in the discovery of the many wonderful passages giving insight into the purposes and nature of Christ, and we worshiped with many beautiful inspirational passages. I also tried to establish the characters of some of the spiritual giants who passed their wisdom to us.

Helping to establish the Community Counseling and Support Service, an interdenominational project in Lamoni, has given me opportunities to serve in agencies and on mental health boards in the whole area of southern Iowa, which includes all of the Iowa counties in Lamoni Stake. This experience has enabled me to see the many personal problems which need our Christian concern and has opened doors for service.

When I sat in the Lamoni Stake delegation at the 1984 World Conference and heard the inspired document read, I felt a tremendous sense of divine power, combined with some fear for the consequences of the move to the ordination of women. I have never heard a more beautiful message than the entire Section 156, and I responded to both the content and the beautiful language. I had made a special study of the revelations given to the church in the past twenty-five years and had seen the constant, steady urging for the Saints to move forward out of a smug, self-contained, protected entity into a world of need.

When the words of paragraph nine were read, I bowed my head in wonder, thanking the Lord for evidence of this concept of personhood. I also thought that I was too old to be called to the priesthood, but I rejoiced in the opportunity to be offered to others. I was stunned and deeply hurt by the reactions of some, making me more aware of how far many have missed the Spirit of Christ and the understanding of the scriptures. I did not even then anticipate the schism which has resulted, although I know for sure that many who have separated themselves through disbelief in this revelation have long denied the divinity of revelations that have sought to move us in becoming more Christ-centered.

I have not really changed my mind about the ordination of women since that time. I have only had the divinity of the move impressed more deeply in my spirit. Some may be surprised at the number of women being ordained, but we must remember the years of service these women have given without the authority of priesthood. Many people have remarked about the quality of women called and the quality of service given. Many of the fears about implementation have been allayed.

I was ordained in the Lamoni Church in March 1987. It was a memorable service, filled with love and the spirit of divine approval. Family members and friends came from a distance to share in this experience with the candidates and the Lamoni Congregation. It was especially delightful for me, as my son came from Sandpoint, Idaho, to share with me. During the ordination I also felt the presence and joy of my deceased husband, Bill, and my deceased father, E. P. Darnell.

Since my ordination I have been blessed with wonderful acceptance by both priesthood men and others in our church. I have also found respect for my ministry by those not affiliated with the RLDS Church. I have had the opportunity to preach in most of the congregations in the stake, to participate in administrations to the sick, to serve Communion, and plan and preside at Wednesday evening fellowship services. The greatest challenge in preaching has been for the Lamoni Congregation, where I have served all of the forty-nine years I have lived in Lamoni. I have stood behind that pulpit untold times, but as I said when I began my first sermon, "This is different!"

I perceive ministry, whether with or without

priesthood, as doing the work of Jesus Christ among the people of the world. It means being sensitive to human needs in the same spirit and understanding that Jesus demonstrated to us in his few years of earthly ministry. It means casting off the restrictive bonds of prejudice and self-righteousness and meeting people where they are—always with the hope of helping them to find fulfillment and peace, but never dictating what they should do. It means seeing our church buildings and our church services as places of preparation to serve, and seeing the real work of the church out there where the "others" are. It means reconciliation instead of recrimination. It means God first, our church second. It means active awareness of world conditions and world attitudes. It means accepting as good and right those parts of alien cultures that add to the concept of the kingdom. It means moving toward "Christ for the World!" It also means developing an understanding of languages that will allow ever-enlarging understanding of the written word and that will allow understanding of the dangers of transliteration without inspiration. It means stewardship of all that we are and can be with the companionship and leadership of the Lord.

I see my ministry as an elder as an increasing understanding of "servant," as a constant but patient urging to greater expectations in worship and daily living, as an agent for education that leads to greater light and understanding of the words and purposes of God, our creator. My concepts of ministry have not really changed in the past few years; they have deepened. I personally have felt greater freedom in investigation, in service, and in leadership, but I feel much great responsibility and much more answerability to God. I see my weaknesses more clearly and have a greater wish to overcome them. I pray that the years ahead will bring us closer to the potential that God sees in us.

Katherine (Snively) Gregory
Portland, Oregon

I have always loved being female. I have been involved in many leadership roles in school, community, and church and have never felt limited because of my gender. I find much pleasure in my responsibilities as wife, mother, and homemaker and also enjoy my present career outside home as a school secretary.

As a high school senior, I was interviewed for a feature article by one of the major city newspapers, and in it I expressed my opinion that one day we would have a woman as president of the United States. As a result of that article, our woman mayor called me to her office for a visit.

Since the early 1970s Saints of the Portland Metropole have encouraged women to assume any task with which they felt comfortable. Only performing the sacraments was reserved for the priesthood. There were, and still are, some people who cannot accept women behind the pulpit. But generally women were not barred from open, active participation in all phases of church life, from pouring concrete to facilitating worship services.

It was within this background that I first began to hear it mentioned that someday there might be women priesthood members. Just as I had felt many years earlier that there was a possibility of a woman being president of the United States, I felt someday there might be women priesthood members. The idea had begun to take root in my consciousness, but I felt it would be "after my time."

Also during this period I realized my marriage of

almost twenty-five years was dead. My husband was an alcoholic, and the conflict and division in our home was intolerable. The decision was made to terminate the marriage even though I am opposed to divorce. It was my firm resolve at that time to never marry again. My parents had objected to the progressive developments at the Metropole and had transferred their membership to a fundamentalist group nearby. This was truly a testing time for my faith. I felt alone, and if it had not been for the support and encouragement of the Saints in the Metropole, I don't know what I would have done.

To overcome the feeling of failure and to fill the empty spaces, I began a program of study. I read the Bible from front to back, studied church history, participated in workshops, went back to full-time work, joined in organizing singles' activities at the Metropole, and assumed responsibilities in areas that my former marriage had prevented.

In the summer of 1981, after several years of "dating," Chet Gregory and I realized that our lives would be even better if we were married. "Our" nine children were unanimously in favor so the following November many friends joined with us as we committed our lives to each other and service to God.

Almost four years later I was called to the office of elder. Rereading my patriarchal blessing, I came across a passage saying that priesthood continues through righteous daughters. I had always felt that it meant my sons would be ordained (and they have been). Now this section held new meaning, and I felt led to ask my father to assist in my ordination. Knowing their struggles, I went to my parents' home and shared several experiences with them. I asked Dad if he would be willing to assist. He agreed, and since then, both of my parents have been able to accept women priesthood members and are personally supportive of me.

I expected to be nervous and anxious the week prior to my ordination service. Instead, I felt calm. I'm sure it was because of the many prayers offered throughout the church.

A television news crew came to church, videotaped the ordination service, and interviewed the ordinands. It was the featured item on the evening news broadcast, and because of it I had many opportunities the following week for witnessing. People came from other congregations around the area to worship with us; the church was filled to capacity. There was such a tremendous spirit present that tears flowed down my face and dripped off my chin. I still have spots on my dress from those tears.

There has been a positive response to my ordination. Even those who reject the *idea* of women in priesthood find it difficult to reject the *person* they've known for years. The only negative item was a letter I received from someone I do not know (not a church member) who wrote a hate-filled letter to me. I have it on file but have dismissed it from my mind.

I am amazed when people seek me out in times of need. Since my ordination, I find my ear is even more sensitive to what people are saying to me. The majority, though not all, of my ministry has been with women and children, particularly in regard to the sacraments—numerous administrations, several baby blessings, baptisms, and confirmations, even ordinations and weddings.

What I find most outstanding is the power I receive from God when I am willing to serve. I find that I am empowered to do many things far beyond my capabilities with God's support and direction, and quiet inspiration comes when I turn to God in prayer. It keeps me growing. I do not enjoy the politics and power struggles that go on in a large congregation. As a priesthood member, I find I am exposed to that element more often than before my ordination.

God and the church have been the important themes of my life since I was baptized forty-four years ago, and I anticipate that it will be so until the day I die. I believe there is a lesson and a blessing in every event in our lives. God hears and answers our prayers. If we move out in faith, doors will be opened, and the path will be in the right direction if we follow God's leading. I look forward with excitement to tomorrow.

Janice (Dandurant) Hawman
Middletown, Maryland

My awareness of my call to priesthood developed over a fifteen-year period. At the beginning there was no definition within my religious milieu for what I felt. But there was something within me that yearned for realization even though it couldn't be defined.

During a conversation one day with a priesthood friend of mine about the subject of women in the priesthood, he said if that day ever came the church would be in apostasy. He said he could see a day, however, when women would be set apart for various tasks. And so that became my definition for awhile. I thought that someday I would be set apart for a certain task. But as the years passed and my conviction grew, I knew with absolute certainty the true definition for what I felt. The Lord had created and prepared me for priesthood service, and my soul was yearning to respond.

I often felt alone through those years. When I married my husband in 1958 at the age of eighteen, he had been baptized only a short time before. Although he remained active for a few months thereafter, he has been inactive since that time. He has not hindered church attendance and activity for me and our two children, but neither has he supported or encouraged it.

One Thursday in August 1985, I went to lunch with my district president and pastor. They interrupted the small talk with the news that I had been called to the office of teacher. I felt torn between joy at the news and terror at its reality. I felt like running away—wanting it so much but not relishing what dealing with it entailed, namely, publicizing it to family and friends. I was strongly aware of my inadequacies, also. If only I could move to another area where no one knew my weaknesses, it would be much easier to handle.

I waited two months for an opportunity to tell my family. An opportune time never arrived, so finally I told them anyway. My husband was accepting, although he made no allowance for any spirituality or sacredness surrounding my call. He was down-to-earth and matter-of-fact about it, reassuring me that he thought I would be good at it. "As much as you've been involved in church, this doesn't surprise me," he said. Yet he did not want this to affect him in any way, for he had no desire to be involved with church activity. He has been comfortable with my call and has not hindered me in my duties.

The following day I told my daughter and son, who were then seventeen and fourteen years old, respectively. They felt it was okay—as long as their friends didn't find out.

Near the end of that week, I phoned my mother in Missouri. "Called to what?" she said. She had no idea what I was talking about. Because of my serious tone and my comment that I was nervous about telling her something, she had thought I was going to say I was pregnant (I was forty-five years old!). After all was clear, she was pleased and said she had no idea I ever desired such a thing.

My great-aunt (who was responsible for my being in this church) and her husband are both vehemently opposed to women in the priesthood, and I knew this. In letters I have received from them, my call is never mentioned.

My sister, who is an inactive member, truthfully

told me her feelings, that somewhere along the way she had learned this was wrong. I could tell, even at the end of the conversation, that she was not accepting of my call. There was no hostility, just a tone of indifference. Recently, though, I have sensed a change, and she seems to be more accepting.

My father, who is a nonmember and divorced from my mom since I was twelve, was totally accepting of my call—proud of it, in fact. He said, "I never knew I would have a daughter who was a minister."

On the day my call was approved, my husband and both children went with me. During the course of that service the lack of rejoicing that I had felt up to that point became inconsequential. During the singing by the choir the Spirit rested upon me in power, letting me know that it was through the Lord's love that I was brought to that day and opportunity. It was impressed upon me that the opportunity for women to serve in this capacity in the church is a divine gift; it did not come about through anyone's efforts or energies.

I am actively involved in a visiting program which provides opportunities to become better acquainted with people and give home ministry. I feel comfortable and at ease serving in the priesthood. I really belong, and I am pleasantly surprised at the strength, control, and authority I feel from outside myself—it's like a gift. I also appreciate the eagerness with which others receive my ministry.

In November 1988 I was ordained to the office of elder. This time, my church family is rejoicing with me, with nearly every member offering statements of confidence and support. This time, I informed my family immediately, without the hesitancy three years before with my call as a teacher. It is with joy and thanksgiving that I enter this new phase of ministry and service for my Lord.

Barbara McFarlane Higdon
Lamoni, Iowa

All my life I have longed for the spectacular kind of encounter with Divinity that many other people report. The Lord has not worked with me in that way. However, as I look back over my life from the vantage point of fifty-eight years, I am aware of the constant presence of the Holy Spirit working with me and for me in many ways. I have been richly blessed with the kind of enabling support that has given me unusual opportunities. My parents' determination that my giftedness should be developed and the strong influence of the church's teaching regarding the stewardship of energy and talent combined to give my life direction.

At great personal sacrifice, my parents saw to it that I attended Graceland College. That opportunity influenced my life in powerful ways. There I found role models, new ideas, personal affirmation, and Bill. I often have thought how different my life would have been and how much less opportunity I would have had if my choice of a husband had been different. My marriage has been the richest blessing of my life.

Because we were blessed with three healthy, outgoing, and independent children, I never was confronted with a choice between my personal development and their well-being. If I had been, there would have been no question that my primary responsibility lay with them. We have had a rich family life while, at the same time, I pursued my own education and profession. When, after Bill and I returned to Graceland to teach, he was asked to become president, I continued to have the opportunity to be part of the faculty—a rather unusual arrangement.

One of the most difficult decisions we had to make was our response to his call to enter full-time church appointment as a member of the Council of Twelve. He was comfortable and successful in the world of higher education and had expected that his contribution would continue to be made in that field. I knew that the new role for him would mean long separations and exposure to personal danger. I had often given thanks in the past that I was not called upon to make the sacrifices I had observed appointee families making. Now I was being confronted by the same deprivation.

My worst fears were realized when Bill's first assignment was an extensive foreign field. I was not at all sure I could sustain the separation. I had not received any specific assurance that I would be sustained in my role as apostle's wife. Yet I was sustained—by challenging opportunities at my work and by internal strength which I can attribute only to the presence of God's Spirit. I remember thinking during that first difficult year, "I can sit at home alone and feel sorry for myself (our children were in college by this time) or I can finally write the book on preaching I have been wanting to undertake all this time." And that is what I did.

I had thought the move to Independence would be our "last stop." Until our retirement I would continue my career in higher education in Kansas City and Bill would serve as an apostle. The invitation from the Graceland Board of Trustees to interview for the presidency caught me unprepared. Bill and I talked it over, knowing realistically that if I became president it would create new dimensions of separation and personal stress for both of us. We finally agreed that it was something I should do. I am very grateful that, once again, I have been supported.

The Lord has never worked with me in ways I would have chosen. I would have preferred to have received clear guidance and assurance "up front." Instead I have gone into new experiences with enormous uncertainty. I have been burdened all my life with a strong sense of inadequacy and feelings of ineffectiveness which have made my response to new challenges all the more difficult. Self-confidence has not been one of my gifts. I long for serenity but it eludes me even though in retrospect I know that time and again a power outside myself has found expression in many different ways through me. Although I have been guided by a "still, small voice," it is still difficult for me to trust its validity.

I believe God gifts human beings to enrich human community. We are called to respond by creating opportunities for the development of those gifts and by finding ways to offer them in service. Many women have felt that this principle did not apply to them. They repressed their giftedness, sometimes as a sacrifice on the altar of supporting other members of their family. We all owe support and nurture to others, but we also owe it to our Creator not to neglect our own gifts. How we manage all this is perhaps one of the greatest challenges of life.

Once at a weekend retreat I was tremendously challenged by a guest minister whose academic attainment and brilliance I had greatly admired. He spoke about the stewardship of giftedness and the world's need for these gifts. Afterward I spoke to him privately, wanting to share my enthusiasm for what he had said. Instead of having my feelings confirmed, he responded by telling me that he didn't think a married woman with children should expect to respond to his challenge. I realized that he had not been talking to the whole group but only the men and unmarried women. I simply could not accept that limitation and felt resentment and anger at being excluded.

As long as I can remember I have had a strong sense of calling to minister. I have never felt that women should be excluded from ordination. In fact, I have used every opportunity presented to me to hold up to women their stewardship of gifts, including their capacity to minister, and to testify that in God's eyes they were not second-class persons because of their ineligibility for ordination. To have excluded a whole group from the possibility of ordination has spoken more loudly to the inferiority of women than all the well-meaning protestations to the contrary voiced by people of influence.

When I first heard the reading of Section of 156, part of me rejoiced and part of me experienced real fear. I felt that this change would distract us from the missionary emphasis of the Faith to Grow program. I also felt that our movement had never come to terms theologically with the role of priesthood. We had put priesthood members on pedestals, making the unordained second-class persons. There was, it seemed to me, a great need to sort out job descriptions for the ordained and the unordained before adding to the priesthood ranks. Ordaining women, I feared, would take pressure off of our need to do that kind of analysis.

As I have lived with the reality of Section 156, I have changed my position in several respects. Although painful, the turmoil in the church has provided a necessary sifting. Many people who have been negative and against any change for years have "selected" themselves out of the fellowship. The presence of some of those, although certainly not all, had held back their congregations and driven away positive people who were tired of obstruction and negativism.

Furthermore, the kind of analysis and discipline I felt was needed in defining roles for ordained and unordained probably never would have taken place without Section 156. We have a long way yet to go, certainly, but we are moving closer as an institution to a better understanding of the contribution of each one than we ever would have if things had stayed the same. There is hope that a careful analysis will lead to the use of the gifts of all who belong to our fellowship.

Because I always have felt women needed to be challenged to be the best they could be, even without ordination, I had some difficulty accepting my own call to the office of elder. I had tried, all of my life, to direct my strong sense of call into available channels, encouraging all women to believe that their gifts were not in any way inferior and that they deserved to be nurtured. I feared that accepting priesthood office would prevent my being able to speak with authority to that large group of women who have accepted their second-class status. I finally accepted my call expecting to continue that ministry.

When my call was presented to the stake conference, the stake president permitted those in opposition to the ordination of women in general to present their position. For about an hour several persons gave their reasons for believing that Section 156 was not the will of the Lord. Some of them were my good friends, and they were careful to say that there was nothing personal about me in their position.

I felt a terrible burden during that hour. I could appreciate the pain of those speaking, but I could not escape the impression that their objections were indeed very personal. Even though I always have tried to focus on my humanness, a part of who I am is my femaleness. The good people who spoke that night were challenging my human worth.

Since my ordination in February 1986,* I have had many stimulating new opportunities for ministry. Traveling for Graceland College has brought a variety of invitations. I have felt a power since my ordination that I did not feel before. That surprises me because I had seen myself as an empowered person without portfolio. I had had opportunity to do many things that an elder does, and I felt supported in those activities. I have a sense now of a sustaining spirit which I did not have before and which has made what I do easier. There is less struggle and a greater feeling of joyous acceptance of the opportunities and challenges confronting me.

I believe that we minister when we allow God's Spirit to use us to meet the needs of other people. That requires putting the needs of others ahead of our own. Ministry also requires development of competence. It is not handed to us without our effort. Ministry is having a passionate desire to share the good news of the gospel of Jesus Christ. Any person who has received that good news can do that. The primary distinction among people, then, is not who is ordained but who is committed.

---

*Barbara Higdon has since been ordained a high priest.

Sue (Kolquist) Jannetta
Mission Viejo, California

I was ordained at the Apple Valley Branch in Minnesota in November 1985. Within five months of my ordination, I found myself transplanted to an entirely new jurisdiction, the Beavercreek Branch in Southwest Ohio District. Here I was totally unknown, among people who had no say-so concerning my call, and I was the only ordained woman in the district. Even though I was willing to go where my husband's job took us, this time it was as though the rug had been pulled out from under me.

My husband Don does not attend any church but has always been willing for me to be active. I appreciated that my pastor included Don when he presented my call and took great care to answer Don's questions. Don was willing that I should accept the call, and because he takes all commitments seriously, he has been supportive in my efforts to fulfill my new responsibilities.

We have no children, so I am on my own when it comes to the life of the church. This situation has many implications for me—some good and some not so good. When we moved to Ohio, I was especially lonely because I couldn't turn to Don for strength and reassurance of my call. I am convinced that if Don were a priesthood member, I would have been assimilated much more easily into the structure. As it was, I felt alone and unwelcome until I was befriended by two women whose calls were pending conference approval.

There are times when I feel a twinge of envy toward those women whose partner in marriage is also a partner in priesthood, but I see certain advantages to my circumstances. For one thing, I can count on Don to put things into proper perspective. He has a subtle way of keeping me from "thinking more highly of myself than I ought." I like not always "talking shop" with him and not being identified just as Don's wife at church. It is my heart's greatest desire as an "ambassador for Christ" that I keep the door open for him to respond to God when the time is right.

Looking back, I see myself as one who slowly but steadily yielded to the enticing of the Holy Spirit. My response to God was fragmented, but it was finally starting to come together at the time of my ordination. In 1970 I was earning a master's degree in rehabilitation counseling. I suppose it's commendable to choose a helping profession, and those counseling skills are of great value to me today. But at that time in my life, my learning came from study, not by faith. I saw no relationship whatever between problems such as chemical dependency, child abuse, and unemployment and the Zionic enterprise. I had the facts but not the commitment or the love to be an agent of change.

Later in the 1970s, I found myself drawn to the writings of such authors as Roy Cheville and F. Henry Edwards—and especially to the scriptures themselves. I felt strongly that I could not belong to a church without being familiar with the writings that were important to its life. Once, on a month-long business trip with Don to Chicago, I decided to make my time alone worthwhile by reading the Book of Mormon from cover to cover and taking notes chapter by chapter. I still use those notes, and it was a powerful experience for me, uninterrupted by phone calls or laundry or the day-to-day mechanics of living.

Next, God worked to unlock my heart, a process which culminated with my patriarchal blessing in 1982. As strange as it sounds, I had been interested in God for a long time but unconvinced that God was interested in me. I prayed almost desperately, "God, I know you love the world, but I have to know that you love *me* and that I can make a difference for you." This prayer was answered abundantly in the experience of the blessing. It was as if I had crawled into my dad's lap and he had said, "Yes, of course I know you Sue, and I love you; I want you to be happy, and I want us to work together." I was never the same person after that realization.

Finally, the doors were opening in terms of activities. This is not to suggest that I had not been active in church. I was an organist, a teacher, a commission leader, and even a bread baker for Commuion. But now I had a new desire to serve God, and I was willing to move out in anything to discover where I could be most helpful. Providentially perhaps, I moved to Apple Valley in 1980, an ideal location for one with my desires. That branch routinely included women in the eleven o'clock worship services.

The first of many experiences for me was giving a ten-minute talk for the lighting of an Advent candle. One year it was my job to plan the Wednesday night fellowship services. These were intimate affairs held in the homes, followed by popcorn, cocoa, and great opportunities for sharing and growing. I first became friends with the women and then with their priesthood husbands, which greatly nurtured and stimulated me. When my call came, I was not really surprised by it.

I used to think that God simply "told" pastors who should be called and to what office. Now I feel that these calls, like the scriptures, blend both human and divine processes. I used to think that power came automatically with priesthood. While I still believe the power comes from God, we must qualify for it through the diligence and faithfulness of our response. I used to think the essence of ministry was the up-front work like preaching and baptizing. Today I place more importance on the inconspicuous, painstaking, behind-the-scenes work of personal preparation and nurturing of others in their quest for God. In at least one arena, my thinking has not changed. The call to discipleship comes to all of us before the call to priesthood. Ordination is not a prerequisite for acting on behalf of the Master in a world that needs everything God has to give.

Upon completing my third year as an elder, I find myself serving in yet another location—southern California. Being a woman priesthood member here is almost inconsequential; my pastor is a woman! Now I must define my role not so much as a woman minister but as a transient minister. Some tasks no doubt fall most appropriately to those who move frequently from one congregation to another. I hope to undertake them positively and adventurously.

Lois (Richards) Kazyaka
San Diego, California

Even as a child I always felt God calling me. A feeling of closeness to God was present even before being baptized at the age of thirteen in the RLDS Church. When I joined the church it was upsetting to me that the priesthood was just for men, for I had been attending another church where women also served as ministers. They had leadership roles and were not just worship participants by playing a musical instrument or singing. But none the less, I joined the RLDS Church with all my being.

When I married John Kazyaka in 1963 he was a nonmember, and we both were in the U. S. Navy, stationed at Bethesda, Maryland. We were married on Friday evening; on Saturday afternoon he was baptized; Sunday he was confirmed; and on Monday he was spoken to under the influence of the Spirit. John and I joined hands in serving God, who has always been first in our lives.

When our daughter, Carrie, was small I again began to question why women were not allowed to function as ministers in the church. As I looked at our children, I was concerned what to tell our daughter. I finally came to the decision that this was a man-made policy and someday it would change. I trusted God to use me when and where he wanted. I would be ready and willing to follow.

A few months before my call and ordination, John was ordained an elder, having served prior to that as a deacon and then a priest. The summer before, a friend asked me what I would do if I were informed of a priesthood call. I told her I would pray, fast, and need a confirming testimony. That caused me to start praying about priesthood once again. Later that summer, during the last worship service of the junior high camp I was directing, I was told by a staff member, through the inspiration of the Holy Spirit, to continue to walk in faith and not be afraid of the changes taking place in my life. I knew then there was a priesthood call for me.

The night before our pastor came to inform me of the call, John and I were talking. I shared with him what offices I felt best suited for—priest or teacher. My heart swelled with joy when our pastor shared my calling as a priest. I realized that from the beginning, God had prepared a way for me.

I was scared about people's reaction to the call, because it was the first for a woman in the Clairemont Branch and the San Diego District to be submitted for ordination. I told both conferences that it didn't matter which way they voted; I was still going to serve Jesus Christ. Both conferences voted unanimously in support of my calling.

I have had opportunity to preach, counsel, serve the Lord's Supper, and participate in the ordinations of three other women in our congregation. It has been a most memorable experience to serve Communion side by side with my husband. For years, I have struggled with our official stance on Communion, and now, as a priest, I find the struggle is even greater. But I know that through this kind of struggle that most ministry is given and changes take place.

There have been times when my judgment has been called into question. In those times my testimony has been that I did what I felt Christ would have done, and I know deep inside of me, with the help of the Holy Spirit, the truthfulness of that statement. My prayer is that I may never view any aspect of ministry as routine or commonplace but that I may always go forward in fear and trembling to serve my Lord and Master.

Ardith Lancaster
Jacks Creek, Tennessee

Whenever I have been asked to participate as a member of the priesthood in any service at church or as a counselor, there has been a greater degree of the Lord's Spirit than I had ever experienced before ordination. This has helped me to understand that there is a definite purpose for ordination. At one time, I was under the impression that even without priesthood, a person who really served the Lord with full purpose of heart could give as much as a person with the added mantle of priesthood. Now I recognize that priesthood is not just a pat on the head in approval for the desire of a person wanting to be of service to the Lord.

While priesthood is definitely servant ministry, it is also the Lord's designation of that person to do a specific function for which there is needed commission and approval. It is the difference between doing the job your own way rather than recognizing the Lord's right to be in charge of what he knows needs to be done.

The concept of servant ministry is a real delight to me. The fact that some priesthood members looked at their priesthood as meaning they were somehow better than others always disturbed me. There was a time when I accepted that as a fact without question, but I am most thankful the Lord spoke through Section 156 on the issue to make clear that self-aggrandizement has no place among the Lord's workers.

After my ordination to the office of teacher in July 1986, I shared the following as my personal response to the Lord's call in my life:

I am nothing in and of myself, but

Where there is hunger, let me be one of the servants, serving the food prepared and blessed by the Master Chef.

Where there is sickness, I would be one of the nurses serving the Great Physician.

Where there is strife, I would be one of the apprentices carrying the tools for the Master Carpenter repairing the breech.

Where there is loneliness, I would be one of the laboratory assistants of the Master Chemist as he mixes the elixirs for filling the void.

Where there is sadness, I would be one of the clowns for the Great Ring Master as he calls for the blending of talents and abilities from all of us misfits, as well as the skillful, to provide joy and diversion.

When there is longing for the Kingdom, I would be one of the ditchdiggers, the laborers, spreading the gravel and tar for the Master Engineer as he builds the highways for Zion.

Where there is craving for self-identity and self-esteem, I would be one of the librarians for the Master Teacher providing resources and materials which help with the discovery of ability and worth and hidden talents.

Where there is desperation, I would be one of the clerks for the Master Lawyer, helping to find alternatives and solutions which can bring freedom.

If I can remember that I have been hired to be one of the servants of the Master Servant of the universe,

If I can remember to always let him give the direction, set the pace, determine the values, and find the real needs,

Then I will be able to avoid the dangers of going off

in all directions at once, of running before him, of choosing inferior materials with which to work, and of wasting time trying to satisfy needs that don't exist.

If I can realize that my vision is limited and His is all pervasive;

If I can be aware that my abilities have come from Him and that He knows what they are and what they were created for;

If I can allow Him to broaden my perspective, to lift me beyond my shallow thinking;

Then will I not miss the opportunities for growth, for refinement, in order to give the most efficient service possible.

This is my prayer.

Evelyn Maples
Niangua, Missouri

The year 1986 was one of the most difficult of my life. On Friday and Saturday, April 25-26, I attended my first Temple School class and was delighted with the quality of the class material and the teaching of it. Here was real vitality, the kind that generated excitement for further learning.

The following week, after a thorough examination by a specialist in pulmonary diseases, my husband was told he had cancer in his right lung. A bronchoscopy was scheduled for three days later, but shortly after we returned home, Bill started spitting up blood. Terrified, I called the doctor and was told to get him to the hospital as soon as possible.

The bronchoscopy was done at the hospital early the next week after the hemorrhaging was stopped. The doctor never reached the offending lung cancer; he found cancer cells encircling the lower extremity of the trachea. Inoperable, he told us. A tissue sample showed the cancer to be one which would not respond to chemotherapy. We were referred to a radiation specialist, and the daily treatments were started before Bill left the hospital. Thus began three months of five-days-a-week, 112-mile round trips to the Springfield Radiological Group.

The doctors were candid about Bill's chances for survival; we appreciated their honesty. We were told that the radiation treatments were merely buying time, but we assumed that meant at least a year or so. Bill died August 7 at home, as he had wished, as I sat holding his hand.

On September 17, which would have been Bill's

seventieth birthday, I received a phone call from my pastor. "Evelyn, you have been called to the office of priest," he told me. "Are you willing to accept the call? I need your answer as soon as possible so that your name can be presented for confirmation at the district conference on the twenty-first."

I had taken the phone call in the bedroom and now sat down abruptly on the side of the bed. My head reeled with the implications of what I had just heard. I knew I could not give an immediate answer. Finally I said, "I cannot say yes to this now. I will call you on Friday."

There had been no uncertainty from me about the validity of Doctrine and Covenants 156. I had known for a number of years that eventually women would be called to the priesthood—but not, I was sure, in my lifetime. And now a call for me? At my age?

My telephone line was busy the rest of the evening. I called my daughter first. "Go for it, Mother," Jo said quietly. "You have been preparing for this all your life." My sons Norman and Matthew were more cautious in their approval. They gave positive response to the call but were concerned that I might assume too-heavy a load. Both were feeling protective of me in the absence of their father. My sisters and brother agreed to pray with me that I might be guided in my decision. And then began the long hours of searching my soul.

I had requested a month's solitude following Bill's death to facilitate the grief process. My children grudgingly acquiesced, knowing my way of dealing with personal problems. During that time I had prayed for direction for the years remaining to me, but I had received no discernible response. Was God now providing the focus for my life?

The questions came much faster than the answers. Why hadn't I had some spiritual experience to prepare me for so awesome an eventuality? The comforting Presence in our home during Bill's last weeks was surely all I needed. And so the seesawing in my mind continued. At the appointed time I called my pastor. "I cannot say no to this call although I have had no personal confirmation," I told him. He thanked me and assured me that others had had confirming evidence. "And remember," he said jokingly, "I'm the fellow who said he'd join the Mormon church if we started ordaining women."

At the Springfield District conference all priesthood calls for women were overwhelmingly approved. Later, my call and the calls of two other women were unanimously approved by the Lebanon, Missouri, Branch, a reversal in procedure necessitated by the time factor. The required Temple School courses were excellent, but I still felt woefully unprepared as November 30 approached. In a beautiful service supported by my family, who had gathered from three states, I was ordained to the office of priest.

I should have ventured forth thereafter full of self-confidence. Instead, even the simplest act of public ministry became cause for painful self-doubt. I had prayed in public most of my life; now I found myself tripping over my tongue. When I was asked to help serve Communion, I rehearsed and re-rehearsed every movement. Perhaps, as my friend and cousin said, I was trying too hard. At the Springfield District family camp in July 1987, the cumbersome self-doubts were lifted. I came to know that my efforts to serve were acceptable and that I would be enabled to do that which the Lord requires of me.

Yes, the year 1986 was difficult, yet the challenges which it presented have filled my days to overflowing. I choose to believe that God knows what he is about in charting the seasons of my life.

Sue (Clements) Massa
Joplin, Missouri

Many things had to take place in my life before my pastor could reveal God's desires to me. I had been a member of the Joplin Branch for ten years and had grown in my association with the Saints in that area. Before that I had attended Walnut Park Congregation in Independence, Missouri, since childhood.

Even though I had always been associated with this church and was raised by good Christian parents, I lacked a faith that stood up to the trials that I created for myself because of poor choices. Because I lacked a personal relationship with Jesus Christ, I ran in every direction but the Lord's, in every storm that came my way.

When I married Ron in 1976 I claimed to be a Christian, but many of my actions were contradictory, and he caused me to question everything I had ever been taught. I began to think for myself for the first time. I was not really sure what I believed, but I did believe in God and felt this church was special. As the years went by, Ron became interested in the church and was baptized. He began to read from the scriptures—his favorite being the Book of Mormon—and would get so excited about the truths he found there that he began to share them with me. Scriptures that I had heard from the pulpit for years suddenly came alive, and I began to read for myself the books I had taken for granted.

A change came over Ron. He was more loving and understanding, so full of faith and patience, and I wanted to be different, too. Ron did one thing that I had not yet included in my daily routine—prayer! We were having family prayer at that time, and I heard the way Ron talked to God about anything and everything. So I began daily prayer—a few minutes at first, but before I knew it, I was losing track of time, feeling the need to pray for others. Prayer seemed to center my thoughts and set the mood of my family.

God became real to me, and for the first time ever I was wanting, with no reservations, to serve God in everything that I did. I wanted to somehow bring glory to God by the way I lived my life. I began to see people differently—precious and special. Even strangers were not just strangers but part of God's creative genius. Everything around me was new and wonderful. Life had more purpose than ever before, and I felt the companionship of Jesus with me continually.

I became aware of a priesthood call for Ron and was thrilled for him. I knew that someday I too might have the opportunity to serve in that kind of role, but for now I was going to be the best member in good standing I could be—with God's help. It was not long until both Ron and I were notified of our priesthood calls. I was not surprised, and yet I was.

Ron and I talked about what this would mean for us and our family—the pros and cons of both of us in active priesthood service. Our children were especially supportive. Our fifteen-year-old daughter was willing to help with her six-year-old brother. This would free up some time for us. I was scared, humbled, in awe of the possibility that God could use anything I had to offer.

Our ordination day of November 30, 1986, finally came, and it was everything I had hoped it would be. Ron and I sat side by side as we were ordained to our first priesthood responsibilities. Ron was ordained an elder; then he stood to assist the pastor in my ordination as a priest.

The reaction of friends and family was varied. Some were not at all surprised. Others thought it was nice. Still others were disturbed by my call and the whole idea of women in the priesthood. I always will be grateful for the strong testimony I had of God's purpose for my life. Without that testimony I could not have survived the rejection I have experienced, even within my own family. My heart has been burdened with the unending prayer that others who desire to know God's will might find for themselves their testimony of Section 156. I continually uphold our prophet in my prayers.

Many opportunities of public service have been extended to me, such as serving Communion and taking it to shut-ins, preaching, teaching, conducting prayer services, and presiding. The work of the Lord is a humbling task, and many times the weight of another's burdens makes me weep for God's children. But I am reminded of God's eternal plan, and I strive to live the "good news." Whether I am grocery shopping, cleaning house, or collecting for the United Way, I am a priest *first*, called to be the extended arm of God's love in the world.

Brenda M. Mitchell
Karlsruhe, Federal Republic of Germany

From infancy I was taught the gospel and to love my Lord. I had the privilege of attending an active congregation in England where the ministry of all people, regardless of sex or age, was accepted. There I was nurtured by the Saints and encouraged to serve. A desire to do what "the Lord wants me to do" has undergirded my actions during most of my life.

In 1962 I went to the United States to attend Graceland College; there I met the man who was to become my husband. When Meredith and I were married in 1963 we made a commitment to serve the Lord through the organization of the church, and both of us have had many opportunities to do so. We lived—and served in the church—in Iowa, Arizona, and Kansas before moving to the Federal Republic of Germany (West Germany) in 1981.

I never saw a need for ordination in my life; I certainly did not desire it. For I had a lot to do as a nonordained person and never lacked for opportunities to express and use my gifts and talents.

Early on in our relationship, Meredith and I agreed that no matter what happened in the church—through all its problems and challenges—if we were in doubt about the path to take, we would follow the prophet. That was seriously challenged in 1984. I never expected the prophet would ever bring inspired counsel to the church opening ordination to women. As I read Section 156 after Meredith brought it home with him from the 1984 World Conference, my heart burned within me as I read the counsel regarding the Temple and the responsibilities of the priesthood; but it plummeted into my shoes when I read paragraph nine. How could the Lord have such a "change of mind"? Why such a change in the status quo? For several days I wept as I worked around the house—doing dishes, making beds, or vacuuming rugs while tears streamed down my cheeks. Tears flowed while I drove the car to work and also while watching television. Why? Why? Why, Lord?

After a couple of weeks I realized my concern over *one section* in the Doctrine and Covenants was hindering me from bringing the service to my family and congregation that I should have been bringing. And so I decided to leave the whole problem in God's hands. There was much to be done, and I needed to be doing my share. I was not going to worry about it anymore until—or even *if*—God decided to call me to the priesthood. Even then, an unshakeable testimony of its validity would be needed.

I continued to pray for a testimony from time to time. But when one did not come, I would lay the matter aside. One day in early August 1986, I was driving home from work, thinking again about ordination of women. As I prayed, a sweet, calm, and peaceful Spirit entered the car. I understood that *if* I should be called, it would be all right to accept. Three weeks later, the pastor of our Stuttgart congregation informed me of my call to the office of priest. I asked for a few days to respond, and after discussing it with my family and praying as fervently as I have ever prayed about anything, I told him I would accept. But where was my unshakable testimony? Must I take a step in faith without reassurance? When it did come, it was a peaceful, calm spirit.

My call was approved by the small German-American group in Stuttgart and by participants at the military retreat in Berchtesgaden. The ordination service in October 1986 was a beautiful experience. High Priest Hendrik Compier of the Netherlands gave the charge to the two of us ordained that day; Meredith's ordination prayer was a moving, yet challenging statement. But still I had not received my dream, vision, or "hand-writing-on-the-wall" experience.

Edgar Holmes, an evangelist-patriarch in England who had been my pastor in Sutton-in-Ashfield during most of my growing-up years, wrote to me and told me I would receive assurance of my call as I reached out in ministry. Several weeks later, as I was reading my patriarchal blessing, I read again instruction given to me as a teenager: when I do those things which are in accordance with God's will, I will have the peace that passeth all understanding. This has been my experience. As I have served Communion to a dozen people in German, spoken in the Netherlands and in England to groups of more than 200, and ministered in both English and German, the spirit of peace was my companion on each occasion.

I am thankful that instead of having one "earth-shaking" experience—which I may have tried to use to persuade others of the validity of my call—that I have a continuing testimony as I serve, guided and supported by the Holy Spirit.

Elaine (Carson) Olson
Porcupine Plain, Saskatchewan, Canada

Although the period from 1970 to now has been one of tremendous growth for me, it would be difficult to pinpoint anything in that time that has attributed more to my ordination than what happened in the earlier years of my life.

My birth was into a poverty-stricken family in a pioneering agricultural area of the Saskatchewan prairie. Our life revolved around the church, except for the mundane facts of life: Dad earned the livelihood and Mom labored endlessly to keep house, sew the clothes, seed and weed the garden, and direct the lives of her family. Walking to school, combating flu and diphtheria epidemics, practicing for Christmas concerts, playing ball, and initiating our own entertainment in a world devoid of radio, television, electricity, or modern plumbing seemed to be only side effects as we rotated around the church, the centrifugal force that molded us.

When we visited our relatives and friends our conversations and our play were church-oriented. We played Sunday school and baptism, and we held mini-preaching services and funerals. Every little chicken, kitten, or puppy that died received the honor of a burial with an attending service. We always opened with "Jesus Loves Me," included "Bring Them In" somewhere on the agenda, and closed with "God Save the King."

As Uncle John and Aunt Nellie Tomlinson, our pastor and his wife, visited with us or the missionaries came to see us, we children listened wide-eyed and open-eared to every word of testimony. To me these were God's men. They were my heroes, and early in life (at least by age six or seven) I longed to be one of them. I wanted to carry God's banner like Moroni; I wanted to be sensitive to God's Spirit calling me to go here or go there as Apostle J. F. Curtis testified so many times. I wanted to open missions like the Apostle Paul and Brother J. J. Cornish. I wanted to preach and to teach. I wanted to be God's man! But, I was a girl!

Mom and Dad brought forth five strong, healthy, wrestling, whistling, outdoor, freckle-faced boys. When it was my turn, they changed the pattern, and I came out a child of a different slant. "Sit like a lady," "Keep your skirt down," "Don't wrestle with the boys," "Brush your hair," and "Don't shout." My sister Alice was my constant companion and Renie a sometimes reluctant tag-a-long. I'm sure we coached baby brother Ken on our version of ministry and admonished him to "prepare." In my deepest longings I envied my brothers.

By my second decade I had stopped asking God to change me into a boy, but even at that tender age I knew effective ministry required learning and developed skills. I studied hard at school. I heard about Graceland College, and a new issue for prayer evolved: "God, help me to go to Graceland." It never occurred to me how impossible that would be for us—poverty on every hand, attending a one-room school offering only up to Grade 8, and an almost universal consensus that education was not for the common herd and especially not for girls. But because of a family move to Regina and the support and encouragement of my parents, I graduated in 1936. Then, with aid from a scholarship fund and a $100 loan from my brother, I was off to Graceland, graduating in 1940.

I eventually moved into civil service with the Royal Canadian Mounted Police and finally into a provincial social work job, which provided as close a substitute to ministry in the church that I could find. I stayed with that until my marriage to Merlin Olson in 1948. In the meantime, as far as the church was concerned, I did what I could when I could. My social work brought me into residence in Regina, Saskatoon, and Weyburn, and I taught church school, joined Zion's League, and studied many books. I participated in or spearheaded many church projects, rallies, stewardship studies, Christmas concerts, and building fund drives. The unsatisfied yearning for ministry was a driving force that led me into tremendously joyous spiritual experiences.

Merlin is a farmer, and after only nine months of marriage we migrated into the pioneering parkland. Farming was just beginning to take hold with the advent of bulldozers and pilers to cut down the trees and pile them into windrows for burning. Our town was small; there were only two RLDS members living in the area, and we immediately contacted them. It was quite a shock to find that starting, building up, and maintaining a church mission was not the dearest thing to their hearts. They did help us get started, though, and that was something to be thankful for.

God didn't spell out the torturously slow growth we would experience, but we have been encouraged many times with the uplift of the Spirit. We held preaching series, church school, rallies, women's institutes, and had contact with the Arborfield Mission. We grew together with them. Our mission is small but not insignificant; eleven relatively isolated members have been held together, have contributed regularly to financial programs of the district, and have at various times held office in district departments. We even bought our church through a loan from the Green Estate Foundation in Saskatoon. Merlin was a priest when we were married and was called and ordained an elder in about 1951. He has been our pastor for many years. We've missed attending only about four Saskatchewan District reunions in our thirty-nine years of married life.

In April 1980 a sudden turnabout in my previous good health occurred. When the doctor explained a cancer diagnosis, I did not panic, but I was stunned. I couldn't sleep as I struggled with the idea of a shorter life-span than I had always hoped for. There flooded into my consciousness a thankfulness for my faith in Jesus Christ. I began to give thanks to God for all my life's blessings, a revelry which lasted for hours. I found rest for my soul and was wrapped in an aura of God's Holy Spirit and the assurance of divine care. That and seven months of chemotherapy got me back on the long road to recovery.

When my district president phoned to advise me of my call as an elder in 1985, I was neither breathless nor awestruck, just joyfully and thankfully happy. Later he mentioned that I did not seem surprised. In all humility, I wasn't. Had I *not* been called I would have been surprised and devastated. After years of a close working relationship with God, with the many times he had blessed me and directed my pathway, and after years of hope, prayer, and preparation, I absolutely expected to be called once priesthood for women was a reality. Some will say this is presumptuous of me, but had the call not come, I honestly believe I would not have had the will to live. I am profoundly grateful for Section 156, but not just for what it has meant to me. Women's participation was an inevitable force that had to be dealt with. The pat answer was that the nonordained could do anything except perform the ordinances. It seemed to me that members of the priesthood would eventually be relegated to becoming sacramental chore boys. Priesthood is much more than the ordinances.

There has been no dramatic change in my life during the past two years. My cancer diagnosis has been narrowed to leukemia or lymphoma, with bone cancer the most likely. The prognosis is "maybe years," with no known treatment or cure. Most people do not know even that much about their future. I have the assurance of God's care, and I just carry on. The mission elected me pastor, but that is no great change. Merlin was pastor and I his assistant; now it is reversed. I can truly say, it's a wonderful life.

Florence Sanford Ourth
Nauvoo, Illinois

When I received my patriarchal blessing in 1926, I was told, "Thou art privileged to live in momentous times, in the day of preparation, spoken of by prophets of old, for the preparation of his people is now on, and you can have a part with that great people if you shall desire to advance the interests of his work in every way." That has been my desire, but I never dreamed it would involve a call to the priesthood.

One morning the telephone rang. My pastor wanted to talk with me that morning, so I invited him to come to my home. A little feeling of uneasiness came over me, but I thought surely not, not at my age—seventy-nine. When he walked in with some papers and booklets, the uneasy feeling diminished as I thought, "He must have come to talk about junior church and children's activities." I invited him to sit at the dining room table where he could spread out his papers. Then he told me he had had a beautiful experience one night in which he had come to know that I was called to the office of teacher; this call had now received administrative approval. I was totally unprepared, as I had had no previous intimation, except for that feeling of uneasiness.

As he began to read to me the specific duties of the office, "The teacher is an advocate of full participation, healthy relationships, and development of a healing, redeeming attitude among the Saints," the Lord let me know these were things I would feel comfortable with and have joy in doing. So I accepted the call and the responsibilities that go with it, trusting that the Lord would be with me.

As I studied the Temple School courses I became aware in a way I had never sensed before of the burden of responsibility put on the shoulders of male priesthood all these years. It was similar to the awareness that came to me when my husband, Arnold, passed away thirty years ago and the responsibility for a family of five sons fell on my shoulders. I had never fully appreciated how he felt. Similarly, I realized that now God wanted women to share this burden.

I was ordained in June 1986 by two of my sons. My other three sons were present, along with my daughters-in-law and grandchildren. I have continued to serve in public ministry such as invocations and Communion talks, but my big challenge has come by being in charge of my congregation's visiting program. I sometimes think of a teacher's work as the example Jesus spoke of, of a hen wanting to gather her chicks under her wings. As a teacher, I would like to gather all under "God's wings" to encourage the full participation of members.

I have had the opportunity to serve not only children and adults in my church and to speak at workshops, but my voice has been used in other ways. When I retired from teaching school I was asked to be a volunteer guide in the Chamber of Commerce Tourist Information Center here in Nauvoo. I have met so many wonderful people who come from all over the United States and many foreign countries.

Once I spoke to passengers from the *Delta Queen* riverboat, a Smithsonian Institute group. Peter Volk, who arranged the tour, said of me, "In Japan there are certain people who are spoken of as national treasures. In my experience of arranging tours, you are one of three that I have met who fit that description." Then the Lord used my voice in still another way when I was asked to participate in a CBS television documentary, "Legends of the Land of Lincoln," with contemporary characters. My segment featured Joseph Smith and Nauvoo and was aired in January 1986.

I find myself experiencing some of this joy with all the people I meet. As I reach out to them, wanting to know more about them and trying to "read between the lines" as it were, I sense how God desires to be a part of their lives. I want to share the joy and peace which has nourished and sustained me all my life with all people, especially those for whom I am responsible as a teacher in the branch. My prayer is that none in my charge will be lost but will respond to the ministry of Jesus Christ and know the joy of living in God's presence.

Leslie Palmer
Independence, Missouri

My husband, Don, and I started our journey together, both spiritually and in service to the church, after our marriage in 1981. We were surrounded with capable, loving people who assisted and guided us in this growth. We each had a deep desire to serve in any way we could, be it cleaning the church, painting walls, stripping floors, teaching classes, or attending Temple School classes. It was wonderful to be needed and a part of a loving group of people.

As a team we also embarked on a spiritual quest for truth, knowledge, and understanding. It was amazing to observe doors opening, books recommended, and people directed into our lives to help us.

One door open for me was working at the Auditorium in the Christian Education Commission. As I descended the stairs from my office on the sixth floor in April 1984 during World Conference, the air seemed charged with electricity, perhaps borne out of expectancy. I took an available seat in the conference chamber balcony, still sensing the charge which seemed to infiltrate every inch of me. The inspired document was read and repeated. For several years Don and I had discussed the inevitability of adding women to the priesthood as well as open Communion. The news contained in this document came much sooner than either of us had anticipated.

I could not remain in my seat as the document was reread, and I returned to my office where I locked the door and knelt in prayer. I asked for strength and fortitude for the church and those who would be called. I offered myself in service to God if that was part of the growth required of me. Previously, I had been persecuted by my ex-husband for joining the RLDS Church and felt I could tolerate any kind of abuse after living through that level of mistreatment.

Several months later, as I sat during the serving portion of a Communion service at Susquehanna Hills Congregation in Blue Valley Stake, I was filled with a power that engulfed and brought me to tears. There was an immediate awareness of its meaning, but I disregarded it as emotionalism. This experience was repeated for three more consecutive months, each during the serving of Communion. Each time I rejected the message, partially out of fear of losing particularly close friends and of what would be required of me.

As the year ended, and having taken on the role of congregational women's leader, I prayed for direction in creating a new structure that would allow for a more flexible organization. What format would best meet our needs? What women should fill those positions?

In January 1985 I awakened about three o'clock in the morning for several nights in a row. I used that time to continue my prayer for the group, our congregation, and the stake. When I was awakened on the third morning, the whole idea, the people involved, and the change in structure were complete in my mind. I got up, wrote it all down, and returned to bed, thanking God for answering my prayer.

The next morning at three o'clock I again was awakened. This time I wondered why. My prayer had been answered. Maybe I've missed something, I thought, so I prayed that my mind would be open, that my thoughts would be freed, and that I would be receptive to further divine guidance.

At that moment I was filled with a powerful love and peace that enveloped me and seemed to raise me above my physical self. My thought processes were on a different dimension, and I communicated with Divinity in an exchange that made normal thought seem adolescent. It was during this dual dialogue that I could not dismiss the call I had felt during the preceding Communion experiences. Questions were posed and answered simultaneously, one of them being my willingness to respond to the call to be a "worker." During this experience I was blessed with a healing of several physical ailments that has freed me to respond more fully to service.

Blue Valley Stake has had a difficult time in accepting women's ordination. Feelings have run high on both sides of the issue, leaving deep rifts or completely severing longstanding relationships. In October 1986 the first priesthood calls for women, including my own, were presented to a stake conference. Twenty-two men and women stood in the Auditorium and shared their testimonies.

As I stood before the conference I became aware of a power and strength that was *in* and *around* me. Though physically having my hands on the podium, it seemed that my right hand was being held at my side by someone who surrounded me with strength and calmness which allowed me a clarity and freeness to communicate my thoughts. Knowing the pain many of my close friends were going through, my prayer was that the testimony I gave would touch even *one* struggling person who was listening. Since that time several have shared how the Spirit touched them as I spoke that day. What a blessing to know my prayer again was answered.

Though the calls of all seven women and two of the men were rejected at that conference, we all have continued to serve with deep commitment, waiting with patience and confidence that God's call for each of us would be fulfilled.

After the 1988 World Conference approved a suspension of rules in Blue Valley Stake, priesthood calls for men and women were processed and approved by congregations. Three of us from the original group joined hands and were ordained together in July 1988 in the Mission Woods Congregation in Blue Springs. We were linked not only by the rejection and long wait but by an awareness of growth each of us has made over the years of struggle.

The process for approval of calls in Blue Valley Stake has been slower than most jurisdictions. But during this waiting period I have learned several important lessons: to be patient; to let go and let God move at a pace not of my choosing; and to respond to that "inner" voice for direction.

We all can make a difference by the example we exhibit in our life's stewardship if we remain positive in our testimony and convictions. I have tried to do this and pray each day that I will grow in understanding as fast as I can tolerate, to step out in faith and share love, and to be a peacemaker wherever I am led.

Amy Evelyn Robbins Parks
Battle Creek, Michigan

To relate the many ways my life has wound its footsteps to the calling to priesthood would be writing my autobiography. My association with the Reorganized Church of Jesus Christ of Latter Day Saints has been the whole of my life.

My mother belonged long before I was born, but that is another story in itself. She was widowed (I was ten) with eight children and devoted her efforts to instilling in us the importance of using our lives in the service of Christ and to always remember the commitments we made to him. Her unwavering devotion, love of Christ and his gospel, and her many sacrifices for us were an inspiration to develop our giftedness to serve both church and community.

I have had the opportunity to serve in the church as teacher, musician, and resource person in crafts, and I have used such skills at workshops, camps, reunions, and in the community. I was widowed after six years of marriage to a wonderful Christian (not of my faith) who encouraged me in my church work. Because I had no children, my time was used to support myself in church and community activities. I worked for sixteen years as recreation instructor and director in an institution for the mentally retarded and enjoyed my work with these special persons.

After retirement in 1972, I had the opportunity to go with a church health team to Honduras and was trained as a dental assistant. I have shown slides and spoken about my experience and the church's involvement there.

I have had many experiences in the church that

tested my commitment to serve the Lord. Many are my testimonies of the joys and sorrows that strengthened my faith in a loving, caring God. It has not always been easy to be a black member in a white congregation. An experience of many years ago, when our family was asked to leave the church for a period of time (because some felt we were impeding the congregation's branch's growth and expansion) left me devastated. We tried without success to establish a mission. When asked to return (we were not the problem) and with apologies from the congregation for the humiliation we suffered, we returned with the courage given us by the Holy Spirit through Jesus Christ. Serving in the church wherever needed and being a representative in the community has been both a source of challenge and happiness.

It was with an indescribable shock of surprise when I was approached by our pastor and told I was called to the office of elder. I questioned the need for a seventy-seven year old to be called when there were those so much younger who could serve without the handicap of impaired vision. Besides, I was already busy in church work. I pondered the call, feeling unqualified, too old and tired, and yet full of wonderment if I could fill this commitment in expanded service to my Lord. After many hours of prayer and meditation, I accepted the challenge, knowing God would prepare the way before me. Many have told me that this call is from God, and their testimonies, with my own, have strengthened me.

I still tremble within at the immensity of what God expects of me and yet know I will never be left alone. My eyesight is fading fast, but I know I can still study and teach a small group that meets with me on Thursdays. I will do my best as a servant of God's people.

Jean Porter
Seattle, Washington

Before 1984 I sensed women would be called to the priesthood. I did not have this premonition because I thought it was true and of God but because I felt the prophet was under tremendous pressures from those who openly campaigned for women's ordination. I was devastated when Section 156 was approved. The prophet had betrayed me. If he had been given a true revelation, I pondered, why did he present the document with the stipulation that the entire document had to be accepted or not any portion of it at all. Why had he not trusted God's Spirit to touch the people?

The next two years were filled with spiritual darkness. I prayed and cried to God for enlightenment about Section 156. Each time a flood of angry thoughts cascaded into my mind and heart. I was so bitter that I could not forgive God, the prophet, or those who had wanted it so badly. The idea of leaving the church entered my mind. But where would I go? I knew I could never return to the Catholic church of my youth, nor could I imagine being spiritually fed in a community church after experiencing the Restoration gospel. The message I received from God when I prayed was that this is Christ's church and he was still in charge. In my frustrated state I decided to wait upon the Lord to bring his wrath upon the wayward Saints and try to worship as best I could.

The priesthood calls of women were being presented for the first time at the Seattle Stake conference. I couldn't decide whether to stay home, go and vote against all the womens' calls, or go and not vote at all. I prayed through a long, sleepless night asking for guidance. No answer came until the early morning hours when the Spirit of God rested upon me. I was reminded of the many times I had raised my hand in support of men's priesthood calls when I did not have a personal testimony of them. I voted because the Holy Spirit was present as the call was being presented and the confidence I had in the whole calling process. The Lord told me to go to conference and be in tune with the Spirit.

During presentation of the calls, I experienced God's loving, gentle Spirit when each name was presented and as each candidate bore her testimony. I could not deny the Spirit I felt, so I voted for every one. With my submission to God's will came the assurance that God meant for women to serve in this special capacity. I also realized my anger at the prophet and others. I was overjoyed to be in tune with the mind and heart of our Lord once again, and I fully accepted Section 156 as God's revelation.

I appreciated the eagerness of women to serve in priesthood capacities but had no desire myself for those responsibilities. God always had allowed me to minister, so when my call to the office of elder came through my husband, Francis (he was the pastor), I was confused. He was filled with excitement and joy. I told him I didn't want or need a priesthood call to serve God. He replied that I may not need the calling, but the people needed the ministry they would receive from me as a priesthood member. He asked me to pray about it, study, and listen to God.

As I prayed and searched, God brought to my mind the experience of the birth of my youngest child, Catherine. I was forty years old when I became pregnant. My thoughts and life-style were geared toward taking care of my four teenagers, and a baby didn't fit into my plans. But when Catherine was born, she was like a magnet, drawing us closer to each other and to God. I decided God desired to bless me as he had done before, so I accepted the call on faith. I knew in time God would give me confirmation.

At the closing service of spring conference, the Spirit of God rested on me and filled my soul. I came to understand that I would fulfill a great need to minister to those around me if I continued in faith and followed God's standards. I knew then that I was created for this particular time and place to share the gospel of Jesus Christ, and I praised God for turning a small amount of faith into a great knowledge of truth.

I perceive my ministry will grow and become a more natural part of my life. At times, I really have to stop and think about being an elder. I know that my ministry is uniquely mine. God wants me to touch others through the same spirit of love that I have received. I'm excited—and a little frightened, perhaps—but always hopeful I will measure up to God's plan for me. May it be for the glory of God!

Jean S. Reiff
Independence, Missouri

My husband and I were adults when we were converted to Christ and his church, and we have always had the greatest respect for priesthood. We have cherished the confirmations that we have received as various men were called.

In 1969 I started working as secretary to Presiding Patriarch Roy A. Cheville. My spiritual life started to grow and expand immediately under the inspiration of a man who was a pioneer in so many ways. I felt encouraged to study and examine long-held ideas and beliefs, allowing the Spirit to lead me in new directions. In 1970 a definite impression came that a woman then employed by the church was a potential priesthood member. The fact that women were not being ordained at that time didn't bother me; I was just pleased that this knowledge had been given to me.

At the time of my call to the office of elder, I was working as secretary to Duane E. Couey. His spiritual maturity was evidenced to me so many times over the years, and I valued his opinion. As we discussed my call, he gave me fatherly as well as friendly counsel and encouragement. My husband was also supportive, although he wanted my acceptance of the call to be my decision. It was only after a few weeks of prayer and consideration that I gave my "official" acceptance.

My ordination in June 1986 by Duane Couey and my husband was a highlight of my life. Our pastor had made good preparation and provided a fine setting. Brother Couey's words and the Spirit present were just what I needed! It was heartwarming to me that so many friends and relatives were present.

I have enjoyed so many beautiful times of ministry that have enriched my life. Our eight-year-old granddaughter asked her daddy to baptize her and us, her grandparents, to confirm her. I was the spokesperson, and preparing for that was in itself a growing experience. The confirmation was both exciting and heartening for me. My husband's "well done" afterwards meant so much. When a man whom I knew to be opposed to women in the priesthood embraced me afterward with tears in his eyes and told me he had changed his opinion, I was overjoyed. Our granddaughter's response to the confirmation was delightful, and we will always treasure her sweet thanks to us.

My first opportunity to serve the Communion emblems was also a lovely experience. Almost everyone greeted me with a big smile, and I will never forget the love I felt for them as I served each one. Administration to the sick has provided significant spiritual experiences, and I have been blessed every time with what I regard as confirming evidence of my call. This confirmation has come as I have moved out in faith, in spite of my feelings of inadequacy.

One of our closest friends was opposed to women's ordinations at first and threatened to turn in his elder's license. But as the weeks went by and he no longer felt "they are shoving women down our throats," he gradually began to change. He responded affirmatively whenever I was in front; he began to smile rather than scowl in church; and then he started *defending* Section 156 at any opportunity. He was one of the first men, other than my husband, to ask me to assist in an administration.

I am grateful to my husband for being my mentor *and* critic. I value his opinion and reaction to things. He has been honest with me as well as kind and helpful. It is a great blessing to have such a companion, and I am sure my priesthood activities have been enhanced because of him.

My concepts of ministry have changed over the past few years. I think of it as ministry offered, not given. I think less of priesthood "ministering with authority," although I do indeed believe in authority. I like the emphasis to be on humble servants of Christ offering to help persons in their faith journey. I think women are bringing a "humble servant" concept to ministry—a caring and a patience that will be appreciated. I believe an excitement is coming to the church as we "stand on tiptoes" to see what great things God has in store for us as we follow, seeking to know Christ better, serving people more acceptably.

Geneva Hunker Richards
Cass City, Michigan

I am comfortable and at home with my priesthood calling; it has brought me peace. To a greater degree than I have ever known before, I have found strength, sureness, serenity, and peace which is abiding and lasting. This peace settled on me at the time I was notified of my call to the office of elder and has been present ever since. This does not mean there has been an absence of conflict or questioning from time to time, but, rather, it rescues me in times of conflict and stress.

I cannot remember a time when I was not aware of God's presence or universality. I was never taught prejudice toward others but rather to love all people. Because of my family's early mission to Norway (my father, E. Y. Hunker, was an appointee), I was surrounded with Norwegian pictures and artifacts, so my mind was exposed early to the larger mission and concept of the church. Even as a child I loved our church and its message.

I was called and ordained at the age of fifty-one. One of my four children has playfully teased me about being a member of the "over-the-hill gang" now that I have entered my fifties. I laughingly accept that, but she will learn that you make it over one hill only to climb another! I expect always to be climbing hills until I move on to other assignments in other realms. Thus, I accepted the challenge of this "new hill" of eldership.

Just before my ordination our district president asked me to consider becoming pastor of a congregation in another town. I accepted but not without trepidation. I contemplated the many years and areas of service to which I had been exposed and all the years of study and leadership responsibilities I had accepted and felt I had a storehouse on which I could draw despite my lack of priesthood experience. My husband had served as pastor of several branches, as district president, and as counselor to five regional administrators and presidents. Traveling with him, supporting him, and also being involved in many of these activities has given me knowledge of procedure and a tremendous background of experience and insight, this has enabled me to move into priesthood responsibilities quite freely and has given me confidence that I *can* and *will* learn.

At the same time I was working on a degree in social work. This came about after my four children had received their degrees, were comfortably employed, and had established their own homes. It also resulted from a need I felt to become better qualified to deal with the problems of unwed teenage mothers, broken homes, confused children, physical abuse, and drug and alcohol addiction as they were working their way into our church families. Accepting pastoral responsibility would mean a fifty-mile round trip added to the 100-mile trip I had driving back and forth to Saginaw Valley University. How could I adequately meet the needs and responsibilities of my schooling, congregation, and district (as women's leader plus codirecting reunion and other responsibilities)? In my contemplation I used the strategy I have always used: If I am needed and what I am doing is for the good of others, then God would be my strength and guide. This has carried me through.

I have been extremely well received by the members of my congregation as well as by the other ministers in the community. I have been serving with the ministerial association—the first and only woman to belong. They have been extremely warm and accepting, and I was invited to be the guest minister at the annual community Thanksgiving service. I used a number of readings from the Doctrine and Covenants and explained to the congregation about this book of scripture. They responded in a warm and wonderful way that I still find hard to believe.

One of my great joys came when I traveled to Independence to visit my mother who lives at Resthaven. She was in a great deal of pain, and it hurt me deeply to see her suffering and be so helpless to provide comfort. Recalling all the years Mother had always been there to bind up our wounds and comfort us, I wanted so badly to provide that same loving care for her. On this occasion she asked me to administer to her. What a great joy flooded over me as I realized I was now able to anoint her and place my hands on her head to talk with God about this wonderful woman who had given so much to my life, to the church, and to others. Who could better present her than one of her own children who knew her so well and understood her faith and need.

Priesthood is a total commitment in accepting responsibility for others. It requires diligence, deep faith, and constancy, and I have been affirmed as I offer my abilities in response to my call to serve. Everywhere, I have found people—in all walks and stations of life and in all faiths—who are offering their lives in loving, Christian service to humankind. I value this knowledge and these relationships.

Mary Kathryn (Becker) Richardson
Puyallup, Washington

Prior to 1984, when there had been talk of *possibly* calling women to the priesthood, I, for the life of me, couldn't figure out what all the fuss was about. Women were just as much a valuable resource to the church as men were. Of course, I could say that because I was not a member of the RLDS Church yet. I had been associated with the church for a short time but was not familiar with tradition as opposed to doctrine.

I had been a member for only three years when my pastor visited me at my home to tell me of my calling as a priest. Needless to say, I was stunned and totally surprised. I told him, "Not me, I'm not ready for this. There are a lot of things about myself I want to change first. Besides, there are women in the church who have been members all their lives who should be called before me." He suggested I take some time to pray about this before giving him an answer, but he wanted to leave with me the fact that several others had confirmed the call.

The following week proved to be one of the most uncomfortable of my whole life. I would start to pray and find I didn't know what to say. I was nervous and jittery; nothing seemed to be going in a smooth direction. For the first time in all this I knelt at the end of my bed, shutting out all noises and activity around me, and meditated for a few minutes. It came to me so clearly that I had been praying for the wrong things—or at least not the way God wanted me to pray. I recalled what I had prayed the previous two weeks: "Lord, if this be your will, tell me or show me a sign." I was led to know God wanted to know of *my* commitment, so I prayed, "Lord, if all these witnesses have verified my calling, obviously it is true and what you want. Therefore, I will accept and commit myself to you."

Suddenly, my life flashed before me. I was taken back to the age of ten when I started to become active in church—singing in junior choir, performing in pageants, accompanying junior choir and playing duets with the organist, singing in senior choir and directing the juniors, and organizing programs. I was developing my leadership qualities while in the junior and senior high band and choir, cheerleading squad, and tumbling club. Even though kids at seventeen regard themselves as mature, they often are still self-centered and can be cruel to their peers. As some of my friends were snubbing or jeering at certain classmates, I found myself to be quite compassionate, trying to set an example for others. Actually, I didn't realize I was like that until the Lord let me see it.

The last fifteen years of my life have definitely had their ups and downs. In the early seventies my daughter was born, and I took her with me to church functions. I became instrumental in helping with the praise singing and open testimony time during the worship services of our "born-again fundamentalist" church. This experience helped me grow and increased my commitment level. Unfortunately, my husband and I were having some difficulties, so I did not have his support for this. In 1977 our marriage ended in divorce. This was a lonely time, but I was sustained by the love of my Lord.

I went back to school by attending night classes for

secretarial accounting while working during the day. This did not leave a lot of time for my daughter, but she seemed to understand. Our time spent together was quality time, and she and I were involved in church work. A year after my divorce, I met my future husband through a dear friend who was a fellow employee at the bank where I worked. Before that time I had never even heard of the RLDS Church, and it took the Lord's intervention for me to see that it was, after all, a Christian group.

Because of my new RLDS friends, I attended an older youth function where I met Terry. After he graduated from chiropractic college, we were married, sold my home, and moved to Washington State to the area where he was raised. Terry was a priest at the time, and members of his congregation eagerly welcomed us home. In my normal pattern of church activity, I became involved along with Terry, especially in music and worship. Three years went by and still I did not get baptized as a member of the RLDS Church. I had been submerged six years earlier as a born-again Christian and could not see the reasoning behind being submerged again just to become a member of this church. However, the laying on of hands was something I had not experienced and was looking forward to it. In April 1982 I finally felt led to be baptized again—this time by my husband as his last official act as a priest. He was ordained an elder a few minutes later.

I continued to be active in the congregation, singing, playing the piano, and being a "confidante" to the members. I was in a singing group along with eight others. Our congregation realized that music was its specialized ministry, and over a period of a few years our group purchased the latest in good sound equipment: soundboard, monitors, speakers, microphones, and miles of cables. What a wonderful experience we have had traveling to different congregations in Seattle Stake and Southwest Washington District to sing praises and share testimony. The response was amazing and so wonderful.

I was ordained on November 17, 1985, at a wonderful, uplifting service full of praise choruses by the whole congregation and much sharing of testimony and prayer. During the ordination prayer, I felt transformed by the Holy Spirit.

It has been a joy to serve in new ways. I feel strongly about the ministry of families and the reconciliation and stewardship for which we in the Aaronic priesthood are called to minister. As I have called for the ministry of angels I have been made aware of the vast power of God. I praise God as I am guided to minister in such situations as there is need.

God has blessed me with a new home and a new baby daughter that two doctors said I never would have. I look forward to continuous service helping people understand the pleasures of sacrificial offering by giving of their time and funds as well as many other opportunities I have to bring ministry. Praise be to God!

Linda Hansen Rounds
Essex, Iowa

I never really felt women would be in the priesthood. Not that I had anything against it, I just never thought it would happen. When Section 156 was brought forth I was surprised, a little afraid of what would happen, but able to accept it readily and with excitement.

From the first word I had regarding this revelation I felt I would be one of those called. I was both apprehensive and excited about the possibilities, and I felt that my whole life had prepared me for that opportunity. As a child, being the oldest of five daughters, I went with my father, Paul F. Hansen, many times when he visited hospitals and took Communion into the homes of the elderly. I saw how he functioned in that capacity and what was expected of him, and early on I gained a special appreciation of the elderly. It was extremely satisfying and joyful that my father and husband were able to ordain me. My father has no sons, and I had always felt badly that there would be no one to carry on in his footsteps in a priesthood responsibility. After my ordination as a priest, it seemed that a part of me that was empty had been filled.

My husband and I had lived in several stakes and in many different congregations, and each time we moved we were allowed to assume new and more responsible positions. I especially was allowed to "try my hand" at a wide variety of jobs and felt that if I tried new things God would help me to grow as a result of being willing to risk.

I've had many opportunities to serve. One of my

first experiences was to give the talk at a baby blessing. After the service many people told me how beautiful it was to have a mother speak on the blessing of little children, because I spoke from a different point of view and brought new insights into that sacrament. Several mentioned the tenderness and feeling that I had brought to that sacrament.

In my calling as a priest it seems I have been given new insights into people. I am more aware and perceptive, almost to the point of "reading between the lines," so to speak, when someone talks to me. I can sense problems more readily sometimes in what people *are not* saying. I'm learning to listen carefully, not so much to give advice, but to let others talk their problems out and see the answers for themselves. It seems too few take the time or the effort to really listen. I feel I need to be more careful of what I say, that now it isn't just my words but I speak in a new way as a representative or witness for Christ.

I am a person who must constantly battle my emotions when speaking in front of people, especially sharing something meaningful to me. When called to serve in my priesthood capacity, this is much lessened. Also the nervousness I feel usually has never been there when preaching—even on two occasions when I had to fill in at the last minute. There has been such an overwhelming feeling of peace and calmness that I am made aware each time that God is with me because that calmness is totally out of character normally.

I am excited about the possibilities for the church, especially for women in their new roles as priesthood members. I see new ways of doing things, fresh new ideas, and a tenderness and caring for people come into play with women in the priesthood. I see women "blooming" and reveling in the new opportunities and responsibilities that come to them. Tremendous growth is occuring in people—both priesthood and nonpriesthood—because of a new dimension in ministry. I am excited about the future and the possibilities that it holds.

Virginia (Bean) Schrunk
Independence, Missouri

My first husband, Lawrence Bean, had been a member of the church but not of the priesthood. Francis T. Schrunk, my second husband, had been an elder. I was a second-time widow at the time I was ordained an elder on June 1, 1986, at an evening service at the Stone Church. The service was altogether beautiful for my new adventure with God, and I felt as if the evening had been planned just for me.

My patriarchal blessing took on significantly greater meaning to me after my call for it seemed to reflect upon the situation. Also, I had received letters from two different stake presidents, one in 1939 and one in 1969, that referred to my work as being of "elder quality." Even though I am sure neither of the men nor myself had any thoughts of a priesthood call, this helped give me the courage to do what God required of me. In the late 1950s, several experiences at reunions and in my congregation were helpful to me in my response to this call.

There were three dreams that seem to have implications of priesthood call. In one, the words came, "You are in this drama of life with the Christ." This challenged me to keep involved with church work. Another dream involved struggling with boulders in the pathway of life. When I came to those too large to get around, I was aware of the assistance of priesthood members. How strengthening that was. Now I, as an elder, would be part of similar blessings for others. Remembering these experiences helped me meet the challenge of my new needs; each brought even richer blessings to me.

A month after my call I attended a workshop conducted by Harry Doty. At the close of the session we were divided into groups of threes to become better acquainted with each other's needs. We were then to petition God on their behalf. One lady was a new friend to me. She took the initiative as we came together and asked to pray. I, a defender of directions given by the instructor, suggested that we were to visit, then pray. She insisted and offered a beautiful prayer for discernment of the other's needs. We then visited. Two of us prayed rather general prayers. When the lady whom I'd never met before prayed for me, she did so with assurance regarding a "power" that was to come to me. I inquired if she knew of my priesthood call. She did not and was not even sure how she felt about women in the priesthood. I told her that her prayer confirmed my call and asked her to consider it a confirmation of the rightness of women in the priesthood.

At the 1986 World Conference, after I had accepted my call in March, I was aware of the quality of ministry the women were giving, while I was frightfully aware of my "lacks." One night at the Conference I felt especially inadequate and struggled with my own capabilities. (This continues to be my concern, not so much in competition but in the realization of my weaknesses when I am called upon to give ministry.) Finally, I felt assured that the Holy Spirit would be available to supplement my efforts. My ministry would be in relation to the gifts God gave me. I could trust God for my needs, for the sake of the people, and for the cause of Zion. I would give my best and have faith.

Many areas of ministry have been meaningful to me, particularly serving Communion, administering to the sick, conducting a funeral, and visiting. Ten months after my ordination, I had the privilege of being with my stepson and three of his children as we were preparing to attend the blessing of another daughter's baby, his first grandchild. I did not know they were planning to have me assist in the ordinance. Tom previously had talked with his older children about it not being right for women to be in the priesthood. At breakfast he called the children to attention and announced to them that he had been wrong. It was right to have women ordained.

The service was beautiful. The sweet new great-grandson nestled in my arms received his blessing through words offered by his paternal grandfather. I was grateful to serve and to know the family would accept the ministry of women as well as men.

To me ministry is functioning in any way that would help further the example of Jesus. It is helping people feel divine love that enables them to respond to God's call. As an elder I find it gratifying to minister to the sick—to administer and to encourage them that they are loved and of worth in God's sight. Sometimes ministry is only presence to support at a point of need.

I can't identify changes in my concept of ministry, although I can see a deepening or enlarging of concepts I held in the past. The opportunities are great and the responsibilities seem heavier when I am carrying them. I think I am now more tolerant of ministers whose time is at a premium when they have a job to earn a livelihood for their families. I may be less tolerant of priesthood who resist training by study and by prayer for ministry in a particular office. I feel any preparation that I can make, I want to make to serve my God whose love is so abounding.

Gael Lynn Self
Chargin Falls, Ohio

I am a convert to the church and was baptized in 1955 in Kirtland. The extraordinary thing about this was that it was the first and only time I was baptized—and I had searched for a close relationship with God from the time I was a young girl. I feel certain that my being brought into the church occurred because of God's guidance and because I was trying earnestly in my youthful way to find God. Once I discovered the church, I realized this was the answer to my search for God, and I have never lost the conviction that this is the Church of Jesus Christ.

My first feelings about the ordination of women were filled with reservations. I disliked all of the discussion at World Conferences with members trying to convince one another of the rightness or wrongness of women being ordained. Why did women need priesthood? Weren't there so many, many ways we could minister in the lives of people without being ordained? However, I soon came to the realization that should the ordination of women ever become a reality, then the only way I could possibly accept such a direction was if the direction came from God to us through the prophet, not by Conference legislation.

What a blessing it was for me to be a delegate to the World Conference at which Section 156 was brought to the church. The Holy Spirit blessed me, and I had the confirmation I needed to know that this was what God wanted for the church and for women.

In March 1987 I was ordained to the office of teacher. During the actual laying on of hands for ordination, I found my mind wandering at first with irritating concerns. Was the microphone going to work? Did my daughter remember to turn the tape recorder on? This mind wandering is one of my faults. Quickly, I realized my distractions and turned myself over to the matter at hand. After all, I was giving myself to God again, in a new way and responsibility. If I were really serious about this, for goodness sake, I'd better attend to what was happening. Never in my life have I experienced what I experienced that evening. I listened to the words of the prayer and felt the beautiful warmth of the Holy Spirit touch me as never before. This intense warmth began at the top of my head and continued to flood slowly from my head downward through my body until it touched all the way to my toes.

Having the support of my family and loved ones in this new responsibility has been an important plus in my life. However, there are some families in my congregation who have not accepted the concept of women in the priesthood—let alone *me* as someone to minister in their lives. This has made me sad in many instances, because some of these people I've known all of my church life. Even though I have felt the sting of their rejection when they have literally turned their backs to me, ignored me, not spoken to me, and said angry things about me, none of these things has made me reconsider for a moment my decision to respond to the calling of God. I do have to say, though, that I have never had anyone abuse me face-to-face for my choice, and I'm grateful for that.

Since my ordination I have been uplifted many times by the acceptance of most of our membership. On a Communion Sunday one young mother said to me, "If you had been serving Communion, I would have moved to the side of the church where you were serving." What a kind expression of support. I did tell her, however, that it was not the responsibility of a teacher to serve Communion but that I appreciated her thoughts.

I have never been comfortable praying in public, but I have been amazed so many times since my ordination how easy it has been to stand in front of people and pray and how my thoughts in my prayers seem to be more organized and more easily expressed. It has surely been the working of the Holy Spirit in making this opportunity to serve in this way so much smoother. I find many ways to work one-on-one with the people, to talk to them, and show my love and concern for them. It is easy for me to encourage people in their attendance, reach out to children and young people to make them feel a part of activities, and try to find areas where individuals can serve. I do not mind being in the background.

My definition of ministry at this moment is simple—it is my responsibility and opportunity to bring the message and presence of Jesus Christ into the lives of people. As a teacher I realize my ministry is most specifically to the members of my congregation, and I like that. Just because people have been baptized and are now members of the church doesn't mean they are in constant communication with God and feel his presence in their lives all the time. Members need to be nurtured, renewed, and refreshed over and over again as they strive to keep close to their Lord. I feel blessed that I have been given the task of "watching over" my congregation.

My professional training has been that of an elementary schoolteacher, although I only worked for a short period of time in the public schools. I have, however, used my training for many years with church school, women's activities, and camps. Experiences in these areas have helped me become more prepared for the ministry I can offer as a member of the priesthood.

I am grateful that I feel no question or hesitancy about the rightness of my calling to the priesthood. In the past months, as our congregation has struggled with acceptance of Section 156, many of us have recognized continuous instances of confirmation of the rightness of this direction. Our worship services have been richly blessed by the Holy Spirit time and time again. That is, perhaps, one of the greatest confirmations.

Karen A. Smith
Ludington, Michigan

The Ludington-Freesoil Mission has a history of having little or no priesthood. Often families were forced to leave our economically depressed area to seek employment. My father served as pastor and was, at times, the only priesthood member until his death in 1970. All this time, it was the women who often held the congregation together. They carried the load.

During my college days I lost track of the church, and it wasn't until after my marriage in 1977 that I again came into contact with the Saints. At that time our pastor traveled about ninety miles each way, every Sunday, just to serve with us. He first suggested to me that I give teaching the adult church school a try. I can still hear him, "Just try it once...." I've been doing it ever since. I never dreamed that the experience I was gaining from teaching and from planning early morning worship services were preparing me for priesthood.

It was when I attended women's retreat for my first time that I began seriously to consider women in the priesthood. We had a special speaker who spoke of the changing roles of women, the full potential of women, and women as ministers. Prior to this, I had avoided thinking about the subject. After all, church policy allowed only men to be ordained. If it was church policy, it must have been correct, right? Wrong! How young and foolish I was. I did not realize that an institution as well as an individual must grow in understanding. At this retreat, however, I was given the opportunity to really think about it, and I became convinced that if the church were to continue to grow towards Zion, this change had to be and that it was only a matter of time. I never expected it to be a reality so soon.

In April 1984 my mother and stepfather came to visit immediately following World Conference. They brought with them the news of the new revelation. I was filled with great, wonderful joy and felt as though a great burden had been lifted—one I did not even realize I carried. The last shackle had at last been broken! We really were equal to and just as worthy as the men. Had I really felt that we weren't? Had I really allowed myself to feel inferior because of outdated attitudes?

All during this time I continued to teach church school. There was, for me, much learning and growing during this period as well as many pitfalls and failures. I found, however, that God was always there to pick up the pieces and was always willing to start over with me.

There have been many changes in my personal life since 1984. My husband was able to land a secure job, which is difficult in our area. It came just in time, too, for our first son was on his way. We were also able to buy a home. Owning our own home was just a distant dream as little as a year before the fact. We were so greatly blessed and so happy with steady employment, a new baby, and our own home.

The world, however, is not a happy place. I began to really take notice of just what is going on in the world. There is much suffering because of a lack of regard for Jesus Christ and for each other. I still cry when I see the plight of little children and ache to hold them all and take away their pain and fear. There is madness in this world, and I decided that I want it to end. It *must* end! There grew within me a great desire to help. I still feel a need to relieve suffering, to dry tears, to make a difference, to strive for Zion. The longing became so great that night after night I would pour out my heart to Christ. I actually begged to be used in some way, any way, to help end the suffering, but I still was not thinking in terms of a priesthood call. When the call did come, I felt a little stunned. (Me, a priest!) However, as I received testimony and encouragement from one person after another, the Holy Spirit touched my heart and I knew this was right and the answer to my prayers.

The ordination service on Easter morning in 1987 was lovely and so meaningful that I'm sure it will always live with me. My mother and stepfather, himself a priest from Sault Ste. Marie, Ontario, came to share in this special day. Even my husband, a staunch nonchurch-goer, was there to "hold my hand." This meant more to me than I can express, but the best was yet to be. I knew I could count on my wonderful, caring mother-in-law to be there, but when my father-in-law entered the sanctuary with her, tears came to my eyes. He never goes anywhere like that, but he came to church for me. There was such an outpouring of love from friends and family, church members, and friends of the church, that my joy could not be contained. I felt the Holy Spirit dwelt with us that day.

Indeed, it is an answer to my prayers. When the job seems a bit overwhelming, I remind myself that I asked for it! I realize now that God has been preparing me for this for many years, and I feel great joy for the opportunities given me to minister. I sometimes experience fear and doubts but receive much encouragement from my husband, family, and friends. Whether they be members of the church or not, they all offer support. We have had another child, and I am so grateful for my family and for so many opportunities for ministry and growth. I have continued to read, study, and explore the ministries of the Aaronic priesthood. I will continue, with thanksgiving, to try to be open to new opportunities of service and will continue to take good care of my family. I am so blessed!

Rosaleene (Coumerilh) Smith
San Diego, California

"If they ever ordain women in my church, I'll leave it!" Those words came out of my mouth one day in 1970 or 1971. We were sitting at lunch in my office at Kearny Mesa Convalescent Hospital in San Diego, California, where I was the social activities director. At the table with me were my right-hand helper, volunteer, and best friend, Lois Kazyaka, and Margi Dillinger Herrick (R.P.T.).

Margi had just mentioned a woman minister in a local church. Margi was and still is active in a Methodist church in LaJolla. A fleeting, unexplainable, weird feeling impressed the moment in my mind indelibly. I passed it off as a reaction to such a dogmatic statement.

As time passed, my friend Lois and I had many good talks about many things, both in and out of the church. We didn't always see eye to eye, but that was all right because we were both exploring, questioning, and testing. No one ever tried to sway my thinking one way or another, but long before the presentation of what is now Section 156 both my husband, Seventy G. Wayne Smith, and I knew that women should and would be included in the ranks of priesthood. I felt we had been "taught by the Spirit."

In my mind I came to understand that "male" and "female" were physical differences of earthly procreation. In the spirit there are no color, ethnic, or sexist designations. I also became aware that ministry is not confined to priesthood, although their responsibility is for administering the ordinances and sacraments. Any individual who cares for another can be used by God to give ministry. "These signs shall follow them that believe" (Mark 16:16). I have also become aware of the gulf that sometimes separates God's truth from human traditions. I realize that, as I look back upon the fallacies of my earlier understandings I can also look forward to an even more accurate understanding of God's nature in the future as I prayerfully study the inspired writings.

I have discovered that God is much bigger than any human understanding and cannot be enclosed in a box of our own understanding and making. I believe that if we free God in our own minds to work in whatever way he sees best, the job of "winning the world" will be accomplished more effectively.

I was ordained a teacher in the Clairemont congregation in January 1987 under the hands of my husband and two of our daughters. Our only son, his wife, their three daughters, and our other daughter formed a family choir. I had been ill most of the month following Christmas, so I was still feeling a little "disconnected," but my feeling of pride for our children overshadowed anything for myself. It was the first time in almost ten years that all four children had been together. It was a happy and joyful day!

I've had no negative reactions to my ministry. It seems that my ordination freed me to act on the insights I have into people's needs as I observe and visit them. At a women's retreat in the spring of 1986 I was given the gift of prophecy, apparently in preparation for the ministry of a teacher. Sometimes, in fear and trembling, I approach someone with a message, but I have never been rejected, received only with warmth and love.

Marilyn Suddaby
Coquitlam, British Columbia, Canada

I like to think that, someday, my great-granddaughters and their peers may read this. For their sakes, I'm glad to have this opportunity to relate how it felt being one of the first women in the priesthood. I hope they will allow me to change my opinions on several church-related topics between the time I write this and when they read it. My views have changed radically in the past ten years, and I suspect they will change again, for I know I am in a time of transition and in the process of questioning.

I have been active in the church all my life. I started playing the organ and teaching church school in my early teens. Since then I have been a choir member, branch and district music director, Christian education director, Skylark and Orioles leader, and responsible for junior church. I have written material for the World Church Christian Education Commission. More recently I have been commission head for pastoral care and Zionic outreach. I was the second woman in our branch to be counselor to the branch president.

Living in Africa for two years (August 1973 to August 1975) separated us from the RLDS Church but introduced me to other Christians. At first we attended the Church of the Nazarene because all the American accents made us feel at home. It wasn't long, however, before we tried the Methodist church and were warmly welcomed. We quickly made friends with several of the English families attending, who were more often Baptists or Presbyterians than Methodists. I think my belief in belonging to "the one true church" began to wobble when we attended Wednesday night study and fellowships in this warm, ecumenical setting. I felt as close to these people as I felt to RLDS members, and we shared together under what I felt to be the power of the Holy Spirit. I remember thinking they would make excellent members of the RLDS Church.

But in one thing we kept apart. We did not partake of their Communion. I think our attitude disturbed them, and they may even have felt insulted. They couldn't understand why we participated in some ways but not in this. I usually played the organ. My husband, Vic, sometimes assisted in planning a service. We were getting close to the point where we would have partaken of their Communion just before we returned to Canada. I respected their ministers very much. But it was not until a few years later that I was bashed over the head with our concept of priesthood authority. Vic and I attended a Marriage Encounter weekend presented by the Anglican Church of Canada. The weekend ended with a Communion service. I agonized whether or not to partake, but when the minister came to me I refused it. As I watched him continue around the circle, I was overcome by a terrible sense of shame. It brought tears to my eyes—as it still does when I recount it. What right had I, I thought, to deny that man's years of ministry? When he and his wife came around the circle again, to wish us farewell, I apologized to him and he offered a prayer of blessing. Since that time Vic and I have been among the instigators of resolutions for open Communion at World Conference.

For several years prior to 1984 I tried to promote, within our branch and district, the idea of women in the priesthood. I talked about it to other women mostly but to men also because I thought people should get used to the idea. I was considered by some to be "bucking for priesthood." At the same time I was involved in discussions about the role of priesthood: Why do we have it? What is the difference between a priesthood member and any other devoted member? I thought of the people who had nurtured and influenced me for good in the church, and most of them were women. I could not see why men who actively participated in branch life were usually called to the priesthood but women were not. If this was the way it should be in God's estimation, then God must regard women as second-class citizens. That was not compatible with my concept of God.

Because I considered women and men equally eligible for priesthood, and when I thought of women who had devoted their lives to serving our branch, I asked myself, Why have priesthood at all? Women have done nicely without it for ages. When I heard Section 156 read at World Conference two or three months later, I was pleasantly surprised. I remember sitting in my delegate seat silently saying, "Thank you, God."

It's difficult to remember thoughts and feelings I had after that. I know I thought that having the right to be called was what really mattered, not being called. I think I was expecting to be called, as were other people expecting me to be. Nothing happened for well over a year. But in December 1985 my pastor informed me of my call as an elder. In September 1986 I was ordained by my husband and my father. What I remember most about the service was the pleasure of assisting Vic in ordaining our sixteen-year-old son, Jared, to the office of priest immediately following my ordination.

I was surprised at my reaction to the call. I was not at all eager to accept. By that time I felt I did not want to be separated from my church sisters in this way. Women had always worked together in the church on an equal footing and now hierarchy was being imposed. I still thought it right and fair for women to hold priesthood if men did (if we *must* have priesthood, then both sexes must belong), but I did not want to be singled out in that way. I was disappointed when my friend and cohort in church activities was not called when I was. There seemed to be other women in the branch with as much or more reason to be called than I. Yet I wanted women in the priesthood to start to balance things out. At the risk of sounding self-righteous, I decided to accept the call as a duty. I couldn't expect other women to isolate themselves from their sisters and not do so myself.

It was a real awakening when on one occasion I listened as ordained women from other denominations expressed how men most often form hierarchies while women tend to be more process-oriented—if there is a job to be done, women get together and do it. Now I related this to our priesthood, which was developed in a male-dominated society. I guess that is why I question our hierarchy of different priesthood offices.

For awhile in church committee meetings, I took it upon myself to explain that men and women do things differently. The men tried to bear with me in a kindly way, but they obviously couldn't see the problem. Some of the women knew right away what I was saying, but not all. I consider myself lucky having the men in our district to associate with in branch and district meetings. I have always felt accepted and appreciated by a large majority of them. We have dealt together with good humor and mutual respect.

I don't think my perception of ministry and priesthood is common at this time in the church. I have been influenced by my husband's explorations in theology and compare his intellectual approach with my father's more emotional approach. I recall previous personal experiences where I thought I was being influenced by the Holy Spirit. While I try to examine those experiences to find another interpretation, I cannot accept my first interpretation without some doubt—but neither can I disregard those experiences.

I still cling to the concept of a God. I am busy rearranging my beliefs about the trinity, scripture, the church, and Christianity—and, of course, priesthood. At the moment I feel secure in my belief that there is no harm in questioning anything that comes to mind. Beneath all doubt there seems to be an awareness of God as accepting, loving, and understanding. I attempt to minister with a vague assumption that God can use me if it benefits someone else. My intentions are honorable. My desire is to help others find joy in life by finding a sense of self-worth, friends, and a decent standard of living. I also wish for them an awareness of beauty.

Those are some of the things I personally have and value. I didn't lose any of these when I lost my belief in the "one true church" or the authority of priesthood. My authority as a priesthood member was given to me by the church body, and I try to work within the parameters of that respected, caring fellowship in such a way as will benefit its members. I think I'm lucky I was born into a church that allows for differences of belief.

Janice M. Townsend
Medical Lake, Washington

Women in the priesthood? I never believed this to be part of the Lord's plan for his church. My life had always seemed rich and satisfying, full of ample opportunity to serve and give ministry. Not being able to hold a priesthood office did not make me feel stifled or unaccepted. When the question of whether women should hold priesthood offices began to be discussed in the church, I thought I was being wise—and very safe—when I said, "I don't think God intended for women to be in the priesthood, but we don't need to be concerned about this. If priesthood for women ever comes about, it can happen only through divine revelation."

Imagine my amazement, then, when that's exactly what happened. I was a delegate representing Spokane District at the 1984 World Conference. As I heard the first words of the document read, I felt the Holy Spirit in great power. At the same time many other thoughts and impressions swept through my mind. I seemed to know that the revelation would be calling women to serve the Lord through priesthood, and I, who had never wanted or thought priesthood necessary for women, was now welcoming it with all my soul. I knew the words were coming and waited with great anticipation. When verse eight was read, it was as if blinders were taken from my eyes, suddenly expanding my narrow vision. I could see marvelous possibilities for additional ministry, rich blessings that would no longer be withheld from God's creation, and strength and power which would be available to the church.

It seemed as though my thought processes were taking place in stereo. A double track was being played simultaneously and the result was an interweaving of the words which the prophet brought to the church and the added insight which the Holy Spirit was supplying. Then the images of various women began to flash through my mind. Each face was accompanied by understanding of what the gift of priesthood would mean in that person's life. There also came the overwhelming conviction that I would be called to priesthood.

Since that experience at the 1984 Conference, the women who came to my mind have all been ordained. I, too, was called to the office of elder in May 1986.

The two years before my call and ordination were difficult ones. I had felt God's call with great strength for more than a year before it was presented to me. It was as if a terrific force was pulling at me, telling me there was a task I should be doing. Yet I had no way of knowing what the task was or how God expected me to respond to it. I spent much time in self-examination, examining my motives, feelings, beliefs, and intuitions. At times I questioned whether there really was a call or whether it was ego which made me think so. During this period I also gave considerable thought to the positions of close friends within the church who did not believe that Wallace B. Smith was speaking prophetically when he presented Section 156. I knew my friends felt sure their viewpoints were right, and yet such opposite viewpoints could not both be correct. I did not want to close my mind to light and direction from the Lord concerning the matter, so I prayed often and tried to remain open to the witness of the Spirit. Confirmation came again and again that Section 156 was indeed God's will for his church. My experience at World Conference was also a source of strength, and I continued to feel that the Lord was calling me to ministry through the priesthood. At first, I had no indication of the office to which I would be called. Then the conviction grew that I would be called to the office of elder. I also received a strong conviction that I would be allowed to serve as a counselor in our pastorate the following year. This later came about.

During this period there were other women in my district and my family who received calls. I prayed about these calls, too, and through the witness of the Holy Spirit it was continually affirmed that the Lord was moving at this time and in this way to bring about his purposes for the church and for the world. The time prior to my priesthood call was painful for me because of the intensity of the call and my struggle to be sure that what I was feeling was actually from God. It was a great relief when the call was finally presented to me. Only then could I find peace within myself. That peace has continued since.

Not all members of my congregation were supportive, however. The apprehension which I and the other women ordinands at Audubon Terrace felt proved to be well-founded. When our calls were made known, several people transferred their membership to another branch. These members were all close friends and even told us, "It's nothing personal." But I felt it *was* personal in that they must believe I have been deceived. They must think I am acting contrary to God's wishes and without his authority.

The challenge of priesthood seems greater for women than for men in that we have no role models or traditions upon which to pattern our ministry. I am not content to simply mirror the dress and mannerisms of male priesthood members. I want my priesthood ministry to be an expression of who I am, and that means there will be elements of the feminine within it. The problem is also compounded by the idea that everyone is watching us and expecting us to do everything perfectly. The thought has been expressed that when new male priesthood members do something wrong, the fault is attributed to inexperience. But when new female priesthood members make a mistake, it is because women really shouldn't be trying to do the job of a man. While this attitude is certainly not that of all persons, it is expressed often enough (sometimes unconsciously) that many women feel pressure to live up to the high expectations of others. In my ministry I have tried not to feel intimidated by thoughts of being on display, by thoughts that everyone is watching to see if I will make a mistake. But the thoughts have been there.

Another aspect of priesthood that makes it hard for women is that many of us already have a full schedule of congregational service. It can be difficult to integrate new responsibilities with old. Priorities must be set and choices made. I am active in Christian education, music ministry, and worship planning and presentation. These ministries are all vital to the life of our congregation and cannot be neglected. Yet at times I have been expected to set them aside because of rostrum ministry. In contrast to these negative aspects, serving in the priesthood has also been exciting and rewarding for me. The power that was conferred through ordination has touched other areas of my life. And the experience which I have gained in my previous church work brings a fresh insight into my new ministry. I am enjoying drawing upon my background in working with children and incorporating this into the usually adult-directed ministry of an elder.

Another positive aspect of priesthood membership has been association with other priesthood members in a new and different relationship. Among the eighteen active priesthood members in my congregation are a retired appointee, two evangelists, one high priest, and the district bishop's agent. These persons, as well as other priesthood members, have been exceptionally supportive and accepting. The first time I stood to preside over a priesthood meeting, I was keenly aware of my lack of experience in comparison to most of those who were there. Yet I also knew that these persons wanted me to succeed. It helps me know that they are willing to do whatever they can to help me function successfully in my priesthood responsibilities.

My experiences as a member of the priesthood have assured me that the Lord is calling all persons to assist him in this work. There is a task for each of us, whether ordained or unordained. I have heard the Lord's call to me.

Ruby L. Ward
Saskatoon, Saskatchewan, Canada

My response to my ordination as an elder in November 1985 was one of overwhelming gratitude to God for his influence in my life: for the loving, Christian family I was born into, for the husband I have been privileged to share my life with, and for the four beautiful human beings who are our children. Now they are successful adults, and our family circle is further enriched by their life partners and our five grandchildren.

During the service I felt vividly aware of all the "divine coincidences" which have shaped my life. My parents were devout members of the United Church of Canada, and my earliest memories are colored by their Christian influence. My only brother became a minister with the Missionary Alliance Church, my late sister was a deaconess for many years with the Community Church at Longview, Washington, and my other two sisters are strong supporters of the United Church of Canada, being active in choir and women's groups.

All through my teenage years I hoped eventually to find an attractive, gregarious life partner who would share my religious ideals, and sure enough, he materialized in the person of Frank Ward. His church, the Reorganized Church of Jesus Christ of Latter Day Saints, was slightly alien to me, and (to be on the safe side, or so I thought), we were married in the Presbyterian church I attended. However, when our first child was born, I was compelled to thoroughly examine the teachings of the church in which my husband was a deacon. We now had the responsibility of shaping the lives of our children, and I considered it important to worship as a family unit. I found out that I had nothing to give up in terms of my belief in God and Jesus Christ; on the contrary, I gained another dimension of divine dealings with human beings on this planet, none of which contravened the New Testament teachings on which I was basing my life.

The events of the 1984 World Conference caught me by surprise. I had not expected the ordination of women to priesthood in the RLDS Church to take place during my lifetime, although I saw it as a natural progression in the church's growth. However, seated as a delegate during that Conference, I felt the overwhelming spirit of the document's validity and a sense of God's intrinsic involvement in our human destiny, individually and collectively. There is a sense of rightness in both men and women sharing the responsibility of priesthood office and experiencing the resultant joys of an ever-deepening commitment to servanthood.

In retrospect, my involvement with the church began with my baptism in 1946, when our firstborn daughter was three months old. In 1950 we experienced the grief of losing our second baby at birth, and the love and emotional support of the Saskatoon congregation made a lasting impression on me. Another daughter and a son widened our family circle. I continued to assist my husband in Zion's League activities and participated in drama projects sponsored by the branch. Later, we moved from Saskatoon to North Battleford where there was no RLDS congregation, and for eleven years we attended the United Church. We sang in the choir, and I was social convener of the women's department, which involved several small groups. Another son was born in 1964. We made many worthwhile friends there and appreciated the spiritual integrity of those who were dedicated to walking the Christian way in the fellowship of that denomination.

In 1968 we were transferred back to Saskatoon, and for a few months we alternated between United Church and RLDS services. Finally, a series of "divine coincidences" caused us to again focus our energies within the Reorganized Church. We have never looked back in terms of commitment and have been richly blessed in our church life. After Frank became district president in 1979, we had opportunity to meet and appreciate many people throughout the district as well as participate in many retreats and seminars. During his ordination as a high priest in July 1980, Frank reached for my hand as the prayer was offered, and I truly felt blessed to be a partner in such a sacred work. The thought of ordination for myself never crossed my mind in any way—I already felt "called" in the office of member.

Prior to my ordination I served in many ways in the branch and district. Yet serving as an elder has opened a new dimension of discipleship and a deeper appreciation of the servanthood aspect of priesthood calling. There is an expanded sense of living for others, of being "a channel to be used rather than a vessel to be filled." I have experienced complete acceptance in this calling from my own family and my extended church family. This has been continued in my new calling as a high priest since my ordination to that office in September 1988.

I was elected to the World Church Board of Appropriations in 1984 and reelected four years later. This led to an invitation to attend a United Nations seminar in New York with the help of the national office of Church Women United. This opportunity to hear from Christian women of other countries and observe the United Nations at work was indeed a consciousness-raising event and underlined the responsibility we have to make the "good news" contagious in practical, unmistakable ways in cooperation with other concerned Christians.

I perceive effective ministry to be a continuing process whereby one becomes transparent to God and to others in terms of spiritual maturity. It involves a willingness to "turn out the pockets of one's mind" to scrutiny before God in prayer. Then into the expectant emptiness comes his divine Spirit, enabling us to fulfill the purpose for which we were created. We are then energized and empowered to help bring about that climate of right relationships between people which we refer to as the kingdom of God. The effective witness of any member—and particularly in a priesthood calling—is predicated on one's prayer life. I have found this to be true and have experienced the ebb and flow of spiritual power in direct relationship to the amount of time I have spent in intentional prayers and in listening prayers.

My concept of ministry relates much more strongly to that of a "towel" rather than a "title." Jesus washed his disciples' feet and dried them. He, who was the greatest and best that human intelligence can aspire to or imagine, demonstrated his supreme lack of earthly pretension, and got God's point across in unmistakable terms. We can do no less.

In 1974 I received my patriarchal blessing. One paragraph, in retrospect, becomes doubly significant in view of the document presented to the church ten years later opening priesthood service to women. It is prefaced by reference to the ministry of my husband, who was then serving as pastor. This is what it says:

"Our Lord will bless your companion richly and bless his ministry richly because of your love for him and your support of his ministry. But in addition to the ministry that you are able to strengthen and help your companion with, in your own personality and your own efforts, God will richly bless you and you will be an instrument in his hands to cause many of his sons and his handmaidens to be much closer to their Lord, and to have greater faith and greater devotion, as you continue serving with such wisdom and strength as you have."

My desire is to live out the import of those words.

Maralin (Miller) Weide
Glenwood, Iowa

No one could have been any more surprised than I was when I was told of my call. My husband and I were told of our calls at the same time. It was the first call for both of us—he as an elder and I as a priest.

It was a difficult decision, not because of my doubts about the validity of the call but because of doubts I had about myself. I had spent much time in study and prayer, wanting a testimony of the divinity of Section 156, especially the part about women's ordination. I attended the ordination of a friend of mine, and at that service I was so filled with the Holy Spirit I could not deny it.

I know, too, that God had been preparing me for this call all my life. I became active in the church in the late 1960s while we were attending a large congregation in Omaha, Nebraska. I had many opportunities to serve and learn there. In 1973 we moved a short distance away to a small congregation in Tabor, Iowa, which had about thirty active members. Five families with small children moved in about the same time. We learned together, prayed together, and worked together as a well-established church family. They were nurturing and patient with us. We also found plenty of opportunity to serve. One very good aspect of this congregation has always been that the work of women is respected and accepted. I served in every possible area open to women at the time. Before Section 156 was received, our pastor already was using women to give invocations, benedictions, offertory statements and prayers, testimonies, and talks. It was well received by the congregation.

Because I attend a small congregation, my pastor immediately put me to work after my ordination. I have had the opportunity to serve in basically the same areas as I did in the past, with the addition of serving Communion, being in charge of worship services, and delivering sermons. The first Sunday I helped serve Communion and also gave the Communion prayers. One woman who had been struggling with the ordination of women said she was filled with the Spirit as I read the prayer; at that point she finally accepted ordination of women.

Added insight into the needs of my congregation has come as a result of my ordination. I have struggled because I feel a greater responsibility and knowledge of how little I know. In the past it didn't bother me to teach a class or talk to the congregation, but now I find it difficult. I feel if I fail, I let all ordained women down. We are being scrutinized by the critics who are hoping to catch us in error. The greatest help to me has been the call of another woman in the congregation to the office of elder. We have supported each other in our unique situation.

My ordination is a continuation of the ministry I have given for the last thirty years. My ministry is and has always been working with the women and their families. Being a priest has helped in my work with them. I have been blessed with guidance, insight, and strength when I have needed it. I have had more emotional ups and downs than I ever have had in my life and feel inadequate and unworthy of the responsibility. I recently told a friend that this must be God's will or Satan would not be fighting me all of the way. I am growing. I do believe it is God's will, and it will make a positive effect on the church and the world.

Dorothy M. Wolf*
Phoenix, Arizona

In 1973 I was serving as women's leader for the Arizona District. Along with a number of other women, our pastor, and district president, I attended a leader's institute in California. It was a life-changing event for me, and I experienced a great spiritual growth through the ministry of those persons teaching. I was reassured through the Holy Spirit during one of the worship services that the leadership of the church was being guided and sustained by God. At one of the sessions the question of women's ordination was discussed, and I was given to know that women would be ordained and that I would be called. I came home and continued to serve and look forward with joy and apprehension for God's revelation that would make it possible for women to be ordained.

As the years went by from 1973 to 1984, I knew with a certainty that this would occur, but as one year followed another I began to feel that the Lord was waiting too long for me. I felt my years of service were on the declining scale rather than ascending. I have served my congregation and district in many areas and received the World Community Youth Award for more than thirty-five years in youth and children's work. I have been active in women's work, in community volunteer work, and had assisted my husband in his priesthood and as a pastor's wife.

All this took commitment and a lot of energy. In 1973 I was fifty-five years old. By the time the revela-

---

*Dorothy Wolf died in August 1988.

tion came in 1984, my husband and I had both retired. He had been relieved of administrative work through his call as an evangelist. So I must admit it was with great relief that the first women were ordained and I had not been called. I felt the Lord and I were in "perfect agreement"—it was too late for me! I was to be a support to the younger women who would be called, and I would give to them unreservedly by voice and action.

But it was not as I had thought. Our pastor told me in the summer of 1986 that the Lord was calling me to be a priest. I must admit I felt a rebellion toward my Lord. I told God it was not my fault that he had been so slow. There were plenty of priesthood in our congregation, so it was not a case of need. I had been teaching, expounding, exhorting, and visiting in the homes of the Saints for many years. (The only thing I had not done was officiate in the sacraments.) However, there was the knowledge that the call was of God, and there was a "Yes, but..." to my arguings: Yes, but I told you I was calling you and my word is sure. Yes, but I need you to be an example to the young priesthood rather than just a support. Yes, but I will give you the enthusiasm and energy you need. And the biggest one of all—Yes, but you promised early in your life you would do whatever I ask! And I *had* found joy and personal fulfillment in trying to do just that. So I was ordained in November 1986 under the hands of my husband and my pastor.

The Lord has been with me and blessed not only me but those of my congregation with a loving, accepting spirit. I have received so much support from my family and my congregation. Those who could not support me because of their objection to women in the priesthood have not openly opposed my ministry and have continued to treat me warmly as a sister and friend. Those in opposition are few in number, and I can see a change in some as they have seen the quality of ministry being given by the women in our area. Other priesthood (young and old) have been especially supportive. Our congregation has had inclusive ministry at our eleven o'clock services for several years with women, children, and nonpriesthood men participating. I'm sure this has been a big help, because they were already used to my being "up-front."

After thirty-five years in the Phoenix area, my husband is truly a "father" to the Metro congregation, and because I have been involved with the children (some are now adults) many consider me the congregation "Mom." This has increased since my ordination with people who need to talk with someone. I'm sure they now feel more open about approaching me because of my priesthood office. I don't know what the future will bring for me or for the church. I've seen many changes in the church, and to me this has been a positive experience, because I have continued to receive assurance (as I did in 1973) that this is God's work and church.

This much I do know: God has guided my life and has helped me do many things beyond my own capabilities. A number of times I have received divine assurance that the Lord wants me actively involved in this work with this people. Therefore, I want to magnify my calling. It is my desire and my prayer to bring ministry to those around me that together we may grow in our faith in God and in his purposes for our lives.

Peggy (Nikel) Young
Saginaw, Michigan

One day when I was nine or ten, I was walking with a friend down the hill between our two houses, talking about church and religion. In response to a remark I can no longer remember, I said, "But don't you want to be like Jesus?"

"No!" she replied with disgust in her voice.

I was appalled and incredulous that anyone would not want to be like Jesus. I always hoped to emulate Jesus through service. It was one of my first confrontations with the "real world."

I grew up attending the Towson Mission in Baltimore, Maryland. My first perceived service began in my early teen years, playing the piano for Sunday services. By the time I was in high school I was also teaching the church school nursery class and serving as Zion's League president. Every summer I went to Deer Park Reunion Grounds to help as a counselor. As a student at Graceland College, I was asked one year to be one of three student speakers at the Lamoni Church on College Day. I prepared that first, short public message with great care and prayer, and although nervous, I thrilled at this exciting opportunity.

Through all those years and experiences I always felt encouraged and nurtured in my gifts. I had important things to do for God, and I felt totally fulfilled in the expressions of that ministry which were available to me. Never once did it occur to me that I was somehow missing out because priesthood service was not available to me. The most important thing I could do was support my future husband in his priesthood responsibilities, which I always hoped would include World Church appointment. This was my desire, and I was frankly glad that I didn't have to worry about the onerous responsibility of priesthood for myself.

Perhaps this is so because in every other aspect of my life I perceived that no options were closed to me because of my gender. I credit my parents to a great extent for that. I always felt in control of my life and able to make my own decisions. I decided to serve God but did not want to belong to the priesthood. I felt happy to serve in whatever ways other people desired that service. I never wanted more than that. As a result, I was truly blind to the frustrations of other women as they struggled for acceptance and fulfillment. I could not identify with the women's movement at all, and I had no concept whatsoever of the tremendous importance the issue of priesthood for women had for many people.

As the years went by I married Leonard Young, and just as I'd hoped, I found myself playing the supportive role as he became more and more busy in priesthood and church responsibilities. Somewhere along the way, however, an interesting thing occurred. I became aware that there *was* a priesthood call for me—as a priest. Mostly, I felt glad that I didn't have to worry about the possibility that this responsibility would ever be realized.

In 1978 we moved to Harrisonville, Missouri, where Len was high school principal. During our years there Len was ordained a high priest and served as pastor. He often told me how it offended him to observe so many capable, competent women in the congregation and not be able to utilize their gifts in priesthood roles. That was the first time I began to think there might be a place for women in priesthood. Those years were a growing time for me. My leadership involvement in several nondenominational and ecumenical organizations forced me to reexamine and reevaluate my beliefs concerning the exclusive nature of the authority of the priesthood and the church. I could not deny that I saw the Spirit of God at work in a mighty way among people of other faiths. I began to examine the scriptures more thoughtfully and found passages which supported my more inclusive views, particularly Mark 9:36-37.

Sometime during those years, I had a subtle perception that my priesthood call had changed from priest to elder. And something else had changed. I still wasn't bothered to think I would never fulfill that call, but the feeling of *not* wanting to serve in that way was gone. I knew I would happily accept such a call if it were possible. In 1982 one of my fondest dreams came true. We were accepted by the Joint Council as an appointee family and began a year of orientation. The wives in the class that year were encouraged to participate in as many of the classes and activities as we could. Eight of us did choose to participate in exciting and stimulating classes. Again, I sensed being prepared for a great ministry, but I never dreamed it might mean priesthood for me. In the spring we received our first assignment and moved to Saginaw, Michigan, where we found the Saints to be inclusive and supportive of ministry from all persons. As the first Christmas approached we decided to go home to Independence to spend the holidays with my parents, who had moved back there after retiring. During that vacation we had lunch with a friend who is a World Church official. That lunch became a turning point in my outlook toward the women's priesthood issue.

He told us of a female friend who was on the verge of leaving the church because it didn't ordain women. I realized for the first time that the church didn't only stand to lose members *if* women's ordination became a fact, but that the church had already lost many members because it *was not* a fact. Little by little I began to discover people whose whole sense of worth, dignity, and purpose had been eroded by the church's position that priesthood was reserved for men only. Each discovery amazed me. I regretted having so casually dismissed this issue just because it didn't personally concern me.

For the first time I began hoping that it would happen for the sake of all the persons hurt and damaged by our exclusive policy and also for the sake of the church which stood to benefit from this vast store of potential ministry. Then came the First Presidency's article in the February 1984 *Herald* about disjunctive revelation. After reading it, Len laid the magazine in front of me and asked, "What does that say to you?"

"It says to me that we're going to have a revelation allowing women in the priesthood," I said.

"That's what it says to me, too," he responded.

We went to Conference that year with happy expectation. I never doubted what was to come until President Sheehy began reading the document at the delegate session. I thought for the first time, "What if it's *not* there." That's when I realized how important it had become for me. I was elated when we finally heard the anticipated message.

I returned to Michigan still not caring whether or not my call would ever be realized. But I found myself becoming more involved in responsibilities I had always considered to be Len's. I had already become a member of the worship commission and learned how to plan worship services. I was serving on the regional missionary commission and later the Zionic relations commission. I accepted invitations to offer guest ministry at district women's workshops and retreats and to speak at banquets and World Day of Prayer services. I wrote articles for the *Herald* which were accepted for publication. The growth I experienced amazed and excited me. I began to consider possibilities I never had before. Something different happened inside me. What never mattered before, suddenly mattered. I *wanted* to be in the priesthood; I wanted to serve in ways priesthood would open for me, particularly in preaching ministry.

Len was the pastor of my congregation. Just as many men over the years have felt ethically unable to process priesthood calls for their sons, he felt that way about processing a call for his wife. I understood that and supported his stance, but it bothered me a great deal to think that my call might not be realized for a long time. What if Len's assignment were changed to an area not disposed to women's ministry, where a call would not be processed? Who knows how long it might be. Many experiences in my own life and also the testimonies of many other people have shown me that God usually waits until a matter ceases to be of overriding importance to a person before he acts on that matter. Such was the case with this.

I struggled with my desire for this call for more than a year. I waited until March 16, 1986. That Sunday Len and I had taken separate cars to church because he had to stay afterward for a short meeting. I took the children home after the service and began fixing dinner. I was standing at the stove when Len came through the door with the letter confirming the approval of my call as an elder. He was so excited he could barely contain himself. And I think it disappointed him that my enthusiasm didn't match his.

Of course, I was thrilled. And not being surprised, I was ready to accept the call. After all, I'd been thinking about it for years. But I was happier to think that I had correctly perceived the voice of God concerning the timing of the call than I was that it had actually been processed and approved. It confirmed to me that I was in touch with the Holy Spirit, and that was the most important thing.

I believe any person can have an experience with God and speak on God's behalf as directed by God. Priesthood places an added responsibility on persons to minister in God's stead. I see it as *potential* for ministry. To say priesthood can bring ministry and nonpriesthood can't is a gross restriction on the power of God to work in people's lives. All persons are required to serve to their fullest capacity in the areas of their giftedness. I see a continuum of potential in the area of ministry. The greater the degree to which persons respond to and are in tune with God's will, the greater their potential is for ministry. But because no one will ever fully understand God's will, we all fall somewhere on that continuum along with others. If any fail to live up to their potential, persons with less ability who respond more fully may appear to have a greater ministry. That's why the word "potential" is such an important key word. But as long as we are moving ahead, that is what concerns God.

And so my journey with God continues. I never cease to grow in my relationship with God as long as I keep moving ahead and serving others. I expect this journey to never end, in this life or the next.

Frances Zender
Millbrae, California

I seem to have been born with a sense of responsibility, so the ministry of meeting needs of people for the past many years has been the kind which might indicate that a call to teacher would be appropriate. After attending a few of our spiritual growth retreats, I sensed a deeper relationship with the Lord which portended more responsibility in the future. I have been doing much of the work of an Aaronic teacher in many aspects for a long time but didn't recognize it as such. I feel my call validated my previous ministry.

I had been in favor of ordination for women for a long time though never considered the possibility of it happening to me. I had thought of it in terms of younger, professionally qualified women who had much to give to the church. It was a shock when the call came to me. I had told my stake president and pastor the day they discussed this with me that I would need a great deal of time in prayer before giving them my answer. That same afternoon, however, I went to my desk, prayed, and read my patriarchal blessing, seeing in it for the first time things that led to this call. There was a "rightness" about this experience. I told the Lord "yes" and was almost overwhelmed with an intense feeling of joy. There was no indecision about my response that day nor has there been in the days since.

Age has little to do with the call. It seems to be dictated by the needs of the people, and I am blessed with a congregation that accepts me and my ministry. There have been needs in my congregation for classes in ushering which I am able to initiate. We have no deacons so there is plenty of work for me to do in the area of teacher and deacon. I have fulfilled some preaching assignments (I prefer to call them talks), and I am in charge of preparing or assigning others to prepare the twenty-minute worship service before each Communion service. I am the leader of the spiritual growth commission in our group and have participated in a witnessing weekend with my husband. There has been opportunity for me to work with persons with a variety of problems.

I have been most fortunate in that my congregation accepts and works with me. Every priesthood member came to me when my call was announced and gave me their sincere support. No one in the congregation or stake has been anything except kind. I know I am blessed in this.

I see my ministry reaching members and nonmembers. Both groups have problems of all kinds, and I help where I can or find the help they need from others. As a teacher, it is essential that I know the backgrounds and problems of others, visit in their homes and have them in mine, to realize their worth and to relate to them in positive ways. Of course, there are the specific duties of the teacher in outward ways, but I feel I need above all to love and help all the persons whose lives I touch.

Before my call, I spread my talents in all directions—teaching, playing piano, writing, visiting—but now I find it easier to focus my energies and talents in specific ways which sometimes include those I've just mentioned. It is now easier to say "no" to some activities. Instead of scattering myself about, I can "center down" and feel more certain of the areas in which I must grow and serve. It is exciting, humbling, and challenging to be helping the Lord in his work at this time and in this place.